# THE HOLY GRAIL
 *a beginner's guide*

## CLAIRE HAMILTON

# Hodder & Stoughton

A MEMBER OF THE HODDER HEADLINE GROUP

# Acknowledgements

The author would like to thank all those who have provided copyright material used in this book.

I would particularly like to thank Danusa Meyer for her illustrations.

Every effort has been made to contact the providers of copyright material but if any have been inadvertently overlooked, the publisher will be pleased to make the necessary alterations at the first opportunity.

Orders: please contact Bookpoint Ltd, 39 Milton Park, Abingdon, Oxon OX14 4TD. Telephone: (44) 01235 827720, Fax: (44) 01235 400454. Lines are open from 9.00–6.00, Monday to Saturday, with a 24 hour message answering service. Email address: orders@bookpoint.co.uk

*British Library Cataloguing in Publication Data*
A catalogue record for this title is available from The British Library

ISBN 0 340 781475

First published 2000
Impression number   10  9  8  7  6  5  4  3  2  1
Year                         2005  2004  2003  2002  2001  2000

Typeset by Transet Limited, Coventry, England.
Printed in Great Britain for Hodder & Stoughton Educational, a division of Hodder Headline plc, 338 Euston Road, London NW1 3BH by Cox and Wyman Limited, Reading, Berks.

# CONTENTS

Eastern origins                                              62
Application                                                  64

## Chapter 7     Symbolism of the Grail     66

The Four Elements                                            66
The Spear                                                    67
The Round Table                                              67
Gwenddolau's chessboard                                      68
The Fisher King                                              69
Pelles or Pellam (see also the Fisher King)                  69
Garlon                                                       70
The Waste Land                                               70
The Castle of Corbenic                                       70
The Grail Maiden                                             71
Feirefiz                                                     71
Prester John                                                 71
The Ship of Solomon                                          72
Sarras                                                       73
The Grail chapel                                             73
Hermits                                                      74
Saint Bernard of Clairvaux                                   74
The Cailleach                                                75
The Castle of Maidens                                        75
The number nine                                              76
Application                                                  77

## Chapter 8     The quest continues     79

Hitler's abortive quest                                      80
The Grail as bloodline                                       81
Beneath the Temple of Solomon                                82
The Templars mysteries                                       82
The hidden Grail                                             84
Application                                                  84

## Chapter 9     The Grail today     88

The ending of the Grail story                                89
The yellow-haired boy                                        90

# INTRODUCTION: WHAT IS THE HOLY GRAIL?

What is the Holy Grail? Is it a cup, a dish, a stone, a jewel from the crown of a fallen angel, a severed head, or a magic cauldron? In the past it has been represented as all of these. But what is it now? Is it a physical object or a spiritual one? Did it ever really exist and, if so, where is it? Then again, why is it being talked about so much at the moment and what possible relevance could it have for today?

The Grail is intensely provocative. It has drawn hundreds of seekers to itself down the centuries. It is the greatest mystery of all and it has not been found.

But today there is a new energy. More people than ever before are being drawn towards the Grail, more writers than ever before are addressing themselves to its mysteries. New evidence is being unearthed, new clues found. There is a strong feeling that we are on the verge of finally discovering the physical Grail but, at the same time, we might have to encounter some of its extraordinary and challenging truths.

Reading this book involves you in a quest. It is a quest that goes back in time to the pre-dawn of history. It is a quest that weaves in and out of the physical and spiritual worlds. It explores powerful and unpalatable ancient beliefs and tracks strange secret societies down the centuries to the modern day. It will prepare you for the finding of the Grail both within yourself and in the outside world.

Expect to be challenged, intrigued, shocked, disturbed, heartened, provoked and enlightened by turns . . .

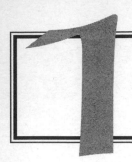

# THE EARLIEST STORY

*Perceval* by Chrétien de Troyes, is generally considered to be the first Grail story, albeit unfinished. It tells how the boy, Perceval, is kept apart from the world by his mother. This is because his father and older brothers, who were all knights in the service of Arthur, have been killed. Grief-stricken, his mother is determined this should not happen to Perceval. She takes him to live in a wild forest near Snowdon in Wales, in order to safeguard him. She orders her servants and the agricultural workers on their estate not to let him go beyond a certain boundary and to keep him ignorant of knighthood. As a result of this he grows up rather naïve and foolish.

One day he meets a group of knights in the forest whose armour glints in the sun giving them such an aura that he thinks they are angels. He lies down and begins reciting his prayers. One of the knights approaches Perceval and, assuring him that he is a knight and not an angel, asks if he has seen some other knights and maidens whom they are following. Perceval ignores his question, and instead indulges his own strong curiosity by asking the knight

Frontispiece for the *High History of the Holy Grail*, Edward Burne-Jones

everything about himself and about knighthood. The knight is
amused and charmed by Perceval's childishness and answers all his
questions. Eventually Perceval directs him to the agricultural workers
who may be able to tell him which way the others have gone.

There follows a strange passage in which Perceval admits he is
unaware of his own name, being called instead 'dear son' or 'dear
brother'. Then he returns to his mother and announces his intention
of going to Arthur's court and becoming a knight. She is appalled
and heart-broken but he is adamant in his decision despite all her
entreaties. At last she has to agree to let him go, and tries to give
him some rudimentary advice about being courtly to women and
serving God. She also tells him the importance of knowing a man's
name. When he finally leaves she falls down in a swoon, but he
rides away regardless.

Next day he comes upon a pavilion and, entering it, finds a
beautiful maiden asleep on a bed inside it. He gauchly puts his
mother's advice into practice by insisting on giving the maiden
several kisses and taking her ring. He then eats and drinks freely of
some pies and wine that he finds. All the while the maiden is
weeping and upbraiding him for his treatment of her, but he is as
oblivious of her distress as he was of his mother's.

Finally he reaches Arthur's court to find a knight in red armour riding away with a gold cup in his hand. He discovers that this knight has just insulted King Arthur and, especially, Queen Guinevere, but he pays no heed to this information, caring only about becoming a knight. Chrétien makes it clear that, although Perceval lacks prudence, he is 'handsome and engaging'. The young man childishly demands the red armour of the knight he saw leaving the court, and Sir Kay suggests he goes and gets it for himself. Arthur reprimands Kay for taking advantage of Perceval's ignorance.

On his way out of the hall Perceval cannot resist greeting a beautiful maiden who is standing by the entrance. She promptly laughs and prophesies that he will be the best knight in the world. This maiden has not laughed for six years. Kay jumps up and knocks her to the floor. He then turns angrily on the court Fool and kicks him into the fire. This is because the Fool prophesied that the maiden would laugh only when she saw the knight who was destined to be 'supreme among knights'.

Perceval then abruptly leaves the court and goes after the Red Knight. Here his naivety works to his advantage because, unaware of standard fighting tactics he uses his javelin against the knight and pierces him through the eye, killing him. Then he takes his red armour and puts it on over the rough clothes his mother made for him. He sends word of his success back to the court and continues on his way, riding the Red Knight's horse.

After this he meets a nobleman who teaches him how to hold a lance and shield and how to fight with a sword. The nobleman is astonished by how swiftly Perceval learns these skills, but Perceval tells him he trained himself at his mother's house using mock shields and cushions. Remembering his mother's advice, Perceval asks the nobleman his name and is told it is Gornemant. At this point Perceval begins to worry about his mother and determines to go home and find out how she is. Gornemant knights him before he goes and tells him to show mercy to those knights who ask it of him and to be more reticent and not to ask so many questions.

Perceval then heads for home through the 'desolate forests'. He comes to a fortress surrounded by water and wasteland. He asks for

hospitality and is invited in by a maiden in a pitiable state who he discovers is Gornemant's niece Blancheflor. That night she comes to his room semi-naked and in great distress, weeping and wringing her hands, and tells him that her castle is being besieged by a knight called Engygeron. Perceval promises to fight him, whereupon she climbs trustingly into his bed and they spend the night, innocently enough, in each other's arms.

Next day, in a tough combat, Perceval overcomes Engygeron but grants him mercy on the condition that he goes to Arthur's court and surrenders himself as a prisoner. He also instructs him to find the girl that Kay struck and let her know that she will be avenged.

The day after, the castle is besieged by a whole army, but Perceval and the other defenders manage to hold out until chance brings them a boatload of provisions. Finally Perceval is challenged to single combat with their leader. Despite Blancheflor's entreaties, he insists on fighting and overcomes his opponent, granting him mercy but sending him to Arthur's court with the same message as Engygeron. After this Perceval is embraced even more lovingly by Blancheflor and she and all her retinue beg him to stay in their castle of Beaurepaire. He insists that he has to visit his mother as he is worried about her, but promises that afterwards he will return.

Meanwhile his captors arrive at Arthur's court and deliver their messages, which are greeted with delight by the court Fool, who prophesies that Kay will suffer a broken collarbone and arm for his treatment of the maiden who laughed.

On his way back home, Perceval finds his route barred by a wide river and is directed by some fishermen to seek accommodation in a nearby castle. He follows the directions and comes to a valley expecting to find the castle. At first sight he sees nothing and becomes irritated, but then suddenly the top of a remarkable tower rises up in the valley before him. It is flanked by two other towers and has a hall in front of it. He enters and is taken to the lord of the castle. This lord, crippled by a wound in the thigh, is called the 'Fisher King'. He presents Perceval with a special sword that can only be broken in one particular circumstance, known only to the smith who forged it. The Fisher King tells Perceval it is his destiny to

receive the sword and treats him with great honour, making him sit beside him. At this point the Grail procession passes into the room.

First a young man enters carrying a white lance that drips blood from its point. He is followed by two very handsome young men carrying gold candlesticks each containing at least ten burning candles. After them comes a beautiful damsel holding a Grail in both her hands which is so radiant it completely eclipses the blaze of the candles. The Grail is of pure gold set with a variety of precious stones. After this maiden comes another carrying a silver carving-dish.

The procession passes by them and into the next room. Perceval restrains himself from asking questions about it because he remembers Gornemant's advice. After this the Fisher King orders food to be brought and they eat. At the serving of each dish Perceval sees the Grail pass before him and wants to know about it. But he decides to keep quiet and ask one of the young lads at the court the next morning.

Next morning, however, he cannot find anyone at all so he arms himself and leaves the castle, just managing to jump clear before the drawbridge is raised up. He rides into the forest, where he finds a maiden weeping over the headless body of her lover. She tells him that the rich Fisher King was wounded in both thighs by a javelin and can now enjoy only fishing. She also reprimands Perceval, saying he 'acted very badly' by not asking why the lance bled or where the procession was going.

There follows a curious passage in which she asks him if he knows his name, to which Perceval intuitively answers that he is called Perceval the Welshman, 'not knowing whether he spoke the truth or not'. The maiden tells him his name is now changed to Perceval the Wretched because he failed to ask the questions. If he had asked them, health would have been restored to the Fisher King and he could have governed the land properly again. She tells him that she is his cousin and that he has failed in this matter because of his treatment of his mother, who died of grief as he was riding away. She then questions him about his new sword and tells him it will fly into pieces when he is in the thick of battle and that it can only be reforged by its maker, Trebucher, in the lake below the Firth of Forth. She then sends him on his way.

Almost immediately Perceval comes across a maiden in a very pitiable state, wearing a tattered dress and sitting on a starving donkey. He discovers that she is the maiden in the pavilion on whom he clumsily bestowed seven kisses, whose ring he took and whose pies he ate, when he first set out for Arthur's court. She has been reduced to her present state by her jealous lover. Perceval meets the lover in combat and overcomes him, making him promise to restore the maiden to her former glory and to take her to Arthur's court and relay the story there. He also sends word again that he will avenge the blow delivered by Sir Kay to the maiden who laughed.

When the pair reach Arthur's court and tell their story, Arthur decides to seek out this unknown 'Red Knight'. Accordingly he packs up the entire court and sets off. Soon afterwards they encamp in a meadow. The night is cold and it snows. Perceval comes into the meadow and is arrested by the sight of three drops of red blood on the snow, dropped from the neck of a goose that was attacked by a falcon. This sight puts him in mind of the face of his beloved Blancheflor and he falls into a deep reverie about her.

So deeply absorbed is Perceval that he fails to notice one of Arthur's knights who has come to bring him to the King. The knight becomes annoyed by his silence and charges him, whereupon Perceval instantly reacts by knocking him off his horse. Kay sees this and impetuously goes to try his own hand against the stranger. Perceval deals him such a blow that he falls on a rock and dislocates his collarbone and breaks his arm, thus fulfilling the Fool's prophecy. Sir Kay is carried back, fainting, to the camp.

Finally, Gawain goes to Perceval and greets him with smooth-tongued courtesy. In this way he discovers who he is. The two embrace and Gawain brings Perceval before Arthur. Arthur learns his name for the first time and says to him: 'Since I first saw you I've grieved over you a great deal; for I didn't know the advancement God had in store for you.'

Great celebrations follow but are abruptly interrupted by the entrance of a hideous damsel who bitterly accuses Perceval of his failure to ask questions concerning the Grail. She blames him for the consequences which, she says, are the continuing distress of the

wounded Fisher King, the widowing of ladies, the wasting of the land and the perishing of many knights. She then takes her leave, flinging out an invitation to a bold knight to find adventure at a certain castle where a damsel is besieged. Gawain immediately responds to this challenge. But Perceval vows never to spend more than two nights in a single lodging until he finds out who the Grail serves and why the lance bleeds. At this point the story turns to Gawain.

Perceval's tale is taken up again when five years have passed. One day he sees a company of knights and ladies doing penance and finds out that it is Good Friday. Realizing that he was unaware of this because he has not worshipped God in all this time, he vows to put this right and goes off to find a hermit. The hermit turns out to be brother to the Fisher King and uncle to Perceval himself. He reiterates what the two women have said about his failure to ask the questions, and adds that it is due to his sin of leaving his mother dead.

The hermit tells Perceval that the Fisher King's father is sustained by a wafer served from the Grail, and that this has been his sole nourishment for twelve years. Then he imposes a penance on Perceval, at the same time giving him some secret names to use for 'our Lord' in times of great peril. At this point Chrétien switches to the tale of Gawain again but promises to return to Perceval later. After following Gawain's adventures for a while, the narrative abruptly breaks off. This is because Chrétien died before completing it.

## application

### Considering the wisdom of the Fool

At the beginning of the Grail story Perceval seems an unlikely Grail hero. This is because he is deliberately depicted as a type of Fool. The Fool is an ancient and important figure and contains within itself many paradoxes. It occupies a prominent position in the Tarot.

In the Tarot the Fool is numbered zero. It represents the Outsider

and simpleton but is also considered the most important card in the pack. The Fool has the curiosity and naivety of a child and is therefore associated with innocence and purity. At the same time he is particularly receptive to receiving unusual knowledge and wisdom. According to the divinatory meaning of the Tarot, the Fool is a seeker of spiritual truth and represents the beginning of a journey. His quest is concerned with discovering the unknown, the inner self, symbolized in this story by Perceval's discovering his own name. Also in this story, the role of Perceval is echoed by that of the Court Fool. In medieval times the Fool was given a special place at court, being allowed to break the rules.

For the student of the Grail legends, recognizing this symbolic thread running through the story is a vital key to understanding its inner meaning. Although Perceval matures and changes through his experiences, he is clearly marked out at the beginning as a Fool figure. The naivety and gaucheness he displays at the opening of the story help to push him out on his journey. It is important to notice that whenever he tries to conform to the norms of society, he is wrong-footed. The great example of this is when he takes Gornemant's advice to curb his natural curiosity. This is disastrous and leads to his dramatic failure on first encountering the Grail. Another example is when he is welcomed at Arthur's court and is about to settle down into the knightly routine when Cundrie the Sorceress arrives and shames him, thus pushing him out again on his lonely quest.

Like the Fool, all who set out on the Grail quest are taking a risk. The risk the Fool takes is that of madness; the prize he seeks is wisdom and inner knowledge. It takes courage to embark on such a quest because the seeker is entering the Unknown. Such seekers will find themselves outside the court, even required at times to break the rules of society. This demands discernment and responsibility. The path can be lonely and challenging. On the other hand there are unexpected helpers on the path. For those who wish to continue the quest, further clues lie in the other Grail texts.

# 2 AN ANCIENT WISDOM

The tale of *Peredur* from the ancient Welsh collection of myths in the *Mabinogion*, is almost exactly the same story. Although Chrétien de Troyes' version of the Grail story is usually treated as the first account, it is not known whether the Welsh version pre-dates this account or was contemporary with it. The existence of the two versions certainly suggests that they each drew on a previous source, now lost. *Peredur* is a much less refined and more pagan version of the story, but there are important differences in it which are worth consideration.

Peredur (Perceval) has found himself at the castle of his uncle, the Fisher King. The King gives him a sword and makes him strike it against a column so that it breaks in two. He then asks him to join the pieces together, which he does. This is enacted a second time and then a third, but this time Peredur is unable to join them up. The King prophesies that he has come into two parts of his strength 'but the third is still wanting.'

After this Peredur sits beside his uncle and two young men enter carrying a 'spear of incalculable size with three streams of blood running from the socket to the floor'. This is greeted by a great crying and lamentation from everyone in the hall. Then, after a short silence, it is followed by two girls 'bearing a large platter with a man's head covered with blood on it'. This is again greeted by a terrible noise of crying and lamentation, almost loud enough to drive Peredur from the castle.

In this account there is no *Grail* as such, there is no radiant light, there are no candles, there is no gold or precious stones. The two most basic elements of the procession, the spear and platter with the severed head, are greeted with great lament rather than awe.

Peredur fails to enquire about the procession but does not find out how devastating the omission of such a question is until the hideous damsel (called the 'Black Woman' by Peredur) arrives at Arthur's court and tells him that because he failed to ask about the marvels 'there will be battles and killing, knights lost and women widowed and children orphaned, all because of you.' Peredur immediately sets out to find the meaning of all this. He has further adventures, which involve playing a magical game of *gwyddbwyll* (a form of chess), and killing a stag or unicorn by cutting off its head. In both of these he is assisted by the Black Woman.

Eventually he arrives at a hall where the lame, hoary-headed man is seated. A young lad with yellow hair says that it was he who was the black woman and he who carried the bleeding head on the platter, and also the spear that streamed blood. He tells him that the head belonged to his first cousin, who was killed by the Hags of Gloucester, who also lamed his uncle. He ends by saying that he, himself, is also Peredur's first cousin. After this Arthur and his men come to the castle and assist Peredur in killing all the Hags of Gloucester.

Although this version has an ending, at first glance it could be considered disappointing. As an explanation of the mysteries of the procession it is, to say the least, implausible. It also suggests a vengeance motif which is less evident in later versions of the Grail story. All in all, the account from the *Mabinogion* is a hotchpotch of

11

muddled themes and fragments. At the same time some of its bewildering material is very ancient indeed. There are strands of powerful symbolism, not least that of the spear and the cup, which hark back to earlier Celtic beliefs and rituals. For this reason it is important to look at Celtic symbolism in the quest for the meaning of the Grail.

# The four Hallows

In Celtic mythology the two symbols, the spear and the cup were connected. They were two of the four 'hallows' or magical objects venerated by the Celts and said to have been brought over to Ireland by the fairy race, the *Tuatha de Danaan*. These were the Stone, Sword, Spear and Cup.

- The Stone was known as the *Lia Fail* and at one time belonged to the powerful King Fergus of Ulster. It was oracular, being said to roar when the rightful king stood upon it. It later became known as the Stone of Scone. The symbol of the stone is connected with the element of earth and therefore with the land.
- The Sword was associated with the element of air. It originally belonged to the Celtic God Nuada. Weapons were considered magical to Celtic warriors and in this respect the sword was oracular. When it was unsheathed it would recount the history of its deeds. Magic swords also figure prominently in the Arthurian legends, the most famous being Arthur's sword, *Excalibur*. The Grail legends contain the motif of a broken sword which the three Grail knights must try to mend. There is another extraordinary sword that Gawain has to find before he can be admitted to the Grail Castle. It was the sword used for beheading John the Baptist, after which it bled every day at noon.
- The Spear was associated with the Celtic god Lugh and with the element of fire. It was famous for its great destructiveness, being the Spear of Lightning. In one account it was originally owned by the King of Persia, who kept it in his palace with its head in a cauldron of water, which continually hissed and boiled. Lugh sent the three Sons of Turenn after it as a penance for murdering his

father. In other accounts the spear stands in a cauldron of blood. A similar hanging spear is found by Balin, who uses it to deal the Dolorous Stroke to King Pelles (see below).

- The Cup was associated with the fourth treasure of the Tuatha de Danaan, the Cauldron of the Dagda. The cauldron or cup was a feminine symbol and associated with water. Water was of great importance in Celtic mythology. Wells and springs were considered sacred entrances to the Otherworld and were guarded by female deities. The symbol of the cup appeared time and again in Celtic myth and the Celtic cauldron offers a rich heritage as a prototype of the Grail. The story of the Spear of Lightning hanging with its head in a cauldron yet again indicates that in Celtic mythology there was a strong link between these two great symbolic objects of the Grail procession.

# Celtic cauldrons

There are several magic cauldrons of Celtic mythology which, taken together, display a variety of special properties. First there was the cauldron of the Dagda, a very ancient Irish deity also known as the Good God. His cauldron provided endless nourishment, but only the brave could feed from it. He himself also had the power of regeneration, being able to strike people dead and then restore them

Celtic head from sacrificial vessel first century CE

to life. This ability may well have been associated with the 'treasure' he guarded.

Then there was the cauldron of the enchantress Ceridwen. It is used to create the magic potion which will confer the gifts of prophecy, wisdom and inspiration on the one who drinks it. Ceridwen brews the potion for a year and a day, intending that its properties should go to her son to compensate for his ugliness. But instead the three drops fall onto the thumb of the boy who is stirring the liquid. He licks them off without thinking and thus is reborn with a radiant brow to become the great bard Taliesin.

A third cauldron, that of Diwrnach, will only serve the brave, not cowards. King Cormac's magic cup is also discriminatory: it will break in pieces if a lie is told over it. But perhaps the most important cauldron story comes from another 'branch' or tale from the *Mabinogion* collection, that of *Branwen, Daughter of Llyr*.

# Bran the Blessed

Bran is huge. He is no doubt an ancient god, but in the story he is the King of Britain. He is visited by the King of Ireland, who requests the hand of his daughter, Branwen, in order to form an alliance between the two islands. This is agreed and the wedding feast is held outside because Bran is too big to fit into a house. However, Branwen's unruly brother, Evnissyen, angry at not having been consulted about the match, mutilates the horses belonging to the Irish contingent. The Irish return in horror to their homeland and Bran tries to smooth over the insult with costly presents. These include a cauldron which has the magical property that any dead soldier put into it one day will emerge the next day restored to life, although without the power of speech.

Branwen gives birth to a son, Gwern, but is later dishonoured because the people of Ireland require their King to avenge the insult of the mutilated horses. When news of this finally reaches Bran he sets out for Ireland with a great army. Bran himself is too big to fit in a boat, and instead wades across the Irish sea. The Irish try to

pacify Bran by building him a huge house, but Evnissyen discovers that they have hidden hundreds of warriors inside it. Again Evnissyen causes trouble. He throws his nephew Gwern into the fire, killing him.

War now erupts and the Irish kindle a fire under Bran's cauldron, restoring life to their dead warriors. Eventually Evnissyen repents and hides among the Irish dead. He gets thrown into the cauldron and stretches out until he breaks it into four pieces, killing himself at the same time. Bran achieves a slender victory, returning with only seven men, among whom is Taliesin.

# The oracular head

During the account of this battle, Bran is called 'Pierced Thighs', but later he says he has been pierced in the foot with a poisoned spear. Bran then commands his seven surviving men to cut off his head and carry it to White Hill (thought to be Tower Hill) in London and bury it there. However, this is not to be done for many years. In the meantime, he says, the head will not decay, but will entertain them just as wittily and well as before it was cut off. So the companions take Bran's head with them and are entertained by it in a place of feasting and birdsong for seven years. After this they are entertained for a further eighty years until a certain forbidden door is opened and they realize they must take the head to London and bury it.

This extraordinary story of Bran ends with the suggestion that the men are entertained by Bran's oracular head in the Celtic Otherworld, a timeless 'Land of Youth' where warriors feast and make merry, a land characterized by the sound of birdsong. This Celtic Otherworld was believed by the Celts to be the repose of souls before they were reborn.

# Preiddeu Annwn

The story of Bran has been linked with what is thought to be the oldest Arthurian story of the quest of the Grail in existence. This is an ancient poem, the *Preiddeu Annwn* ('Spoils of the Underworld'), said to be written by Taliesin. It tells how Arthur and his warriors voyage to the Otherwordly kingdom of Annwn in search of a magic pearl-rimmed cauldron guarded by nine Celtic priestesses, who warm it with their breath. The journey is extremely perilous. The warriors sail in an enchanted ship called *Prydwen* (Fair Face) and have to survive seven challenges relating to seven different castles, located in Annwn. Finally only seven of the warriors return, including Taliesin, and it is not known whether they bring the cauldron back with them or not:

> *In Caer Pedryvan, four times revolving,*
> *We came upon the Cauldron of Annwn*
> *With a ridge around its edge of pearls.*
> *By the breath of nine muses was it warmed,*
> *Nor will it boil the food of a coward.*
> *Before Hell's portals lights were burning,*
> *And when we went with Arthur, of splendid endeavour,*
> *Except seven, none returned from Caer Veddwid.*[1]

# The cult of the head

The extraordinary story of the Oracular Head of Bran is linked to the Celtic veneration of the head. The Celts believed that it contained the soul. The head of an important and brave enemy would often be severed and kept by a Celtic warrior for its magical properties. Usually the brains were replaced with a lime mixture, or the head would be preserved with oil. Sometimes the head would then be lined with gold or lead and used as a drinking cup. Perhaps it was believed that in this way the character traits or virtues formerly possessed by the owner of the head would pass to the triumphant warrior. Certainly it was the custom for kings and heroes to 'consult'

the head of a dead warrior or ancestor. This was what Arthur claimed he was doing when he had the head of Bran dug up, but his real reason was to replace Bran as Protector of the land.

# The Maimed King

The languishing of the wounded Fisher King is another extraordinary motif in the legend of the Grail. Again, early Celtic belief and ritual may be able to throw light on it. The Celts believed in the all-encompassing power of the Great Goddess who was Nature, or the earth itself. It was she who nourished and sustained all life. As her consort, the King was responsible for ensuring her fertility and thus the fertility of the land. The fruitfulness of the earth therefore depended on the King's state of health. If he was wounded or disfigured the earth would suffer. To prevent this, every year there was a ritual enactment of the hero being challenged by a new, lustier hero who would fight him for the Goddess. This was symbolically linked to the seasons and could be seen as Summer wresting the Goddess, Spring, from the clutches of the old King of Winter.

In the legend of the Grail the Fisher King is said to be wounded in one or both of his thighs. This is considered a euphemism for the genitals. In other words, he is impotent. Accordingly he is surrounded by a Waste Land. It is made clear that the healing of the King will bring about the healing of the land. The masculine symbol of the bleeding spear, taken together with the female symbol of the Grail as vessel, could also be seen as denoting the organs of generation and fertility. The spear is maimed and cannot fertilize the land.

The task of the Grail questor is to ask the Ritual Question which will ensure the healing (or death) of the King, so that either he or the questor can take on the proper role of kingship and restore the land to health.

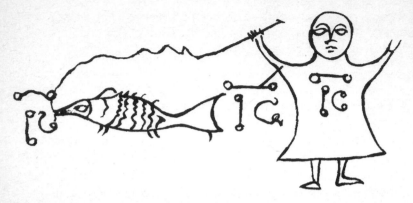

*Jesus the Fisherman* Coptic magic papyrus, Egypt

# The Cailleach or the Dark Goddess

There is an early Celtic story of Niall of Ireland who, alone of his companions, is prepared to kiss a loathsome black hag who guards a well. She is transformed by his kiss into a beautiful queen. She informs him that she is the Sovereign of all Ireland. Then she makes him her consort and bestows on him the kingship of Tara.

The Dark Goddess, or *Cailleach* is a type of sovereignty, she is also known as the Grey Hag, Black Annis or the Hag of Beare. In *Peredur* she is called 'the Black Woman'. (In a later version of the story she is called Cundrie the Sorceress.) It is she who appears at Arthur's court and berates Perceval for not asking the question. She is the dark side of the Great Goddess whose role it is to harry the hero into attaining his full powers. Certainly it is she who makes him take up the quest again and her role is developed in later versions of the Grail where she leads Perceval into crucial further stages of the quest. (See also Chapter 7.)

# The Damsels of the Wells

Before we leave the stories of the Celts and the powerful symbolic background they provide, with their hints of ancient ritual and secret wisdom, it is worth examining a curious tale which, although written after the *Mabinogion*, claims to be the myth which precedes the story of the Grail. This is the *Elucidation*, thought to be written around 1315, in which the author, who calls himself Master Bleheris, offers to tell how the rich land of Logres (Britain) came to be wasted.

He says that in ancient times all the wells of the land were attended by damsels who would provide meat and drink to all weary knights and travellers on their journeys. These refreshments were served from a cup of gold and a dish of gold or silver. Each traveller would be given food that pleased him. But one day the evil King Amangons abused this custom. Although as King it was his duty to protect the damsels, instead he raped one of them and carried off her cup of gold. After this his vassals did the same, until the damsels disappeared from the wells, which then dried up and the land with them.

> *The meadows and the flowers were dried up and the waters were shrunken, nor as then might no man find the Court of the Rich Fisherman that wont to make in the land a glittering glory of gold and silver, of ermines and minever, of rich palls of sendal, of meats and of stuffs, of falcons gentle and merlins and tercels and sparrow-hawks and falcons peregrine.* [2]

After this, when King Arthur formed his company of the Round Table, his knights were determined to recover the wells and reinstate and protect the damsels. The damsels they went to rescue in the forests turned out to be descendants of the damsels of the wells. These descendants were also responsible for building the Castle of Maidens (see Chapter 7). Not surprisingly the evil knights who were imprisoning the damsels were descended from those who had raped them. It was these whom Arthur and his knights challenged and killed.

This story is suggestive of the female deities, guardians of the springs which were sacred to the Celts and were considered the gateways to the Otherworld. Jessie Weston in *From Ritual to Romance* thinks this story relates to an ancient nature ritual performed by priestesses which became disregarded, after which a drought occurred. Whether this was the case or not, the story of the Damsels of the Wells is certainly a parable of the dishonouring of the Earth Mother.

# application

## Crossing the waste Land

*When my tutor described it to me, it sounded strange*
*But now I am here, with the grit of it filling my shoes,*
*I find that the worst thing about it is this:*
*The desert is something familiar.*[3]

The Celts believed that spiritual truth was composed of dark and light aspects. They also believed that the darkness preceded the light. This reflected their understanding that death had to precede rebirth. The Celtic year, therefore, began at the onset of winter. Similarly their days began with the night (as in fortnight). Their most revered deity, the Great Goddess, had a dark face as well as one of light.

The Grail quest often begins in the darkness and desolation of the Waste Land. It is a place which is strange and frightening yet at the same time horribly familiar. Poets have been there and spoken of it powerfully in verse. Saints have called it the Dark Night of the Soul; psychoanalysts have seen it as depression. It is a place of spiritual and emotional aridity.

## Visualization

You are in the middle of the Waste Land. All around you is featureless landscape; sand lies beneath your feet. No greenery

can be seen, only dry roots, stones and rubbish. The sun beats down and nothing gives shade. You know you cannot go back because the way is barred. You can only go forward and you are not certain that you will survive. You cannot even remember why you set out. The wind moans in your ears, carrying familiar voices of discouragement. Mirages appear before you of people and things that you have no wish to remember.

It has taken courage for you to arrive here. At some level you know this, but emotionally you cannot reach that knowledge. You trudge on with no hope of relief. You long for water and for company. You remember that others have been here ahead of you and that somewhere there will be an end, perhaps a dark tower, a horn to blow, a knight to challenge you.

Now the landscape begins to change, hills appear and mass up into mountains, a bell begins to toll. You trudge on, parched, your eyes dry in their sockets. A dark shape looms up. It is a tower like the tower of the Grail Castle itself. As you press on with dread towards it, it seems to recede. Then all at once it is directly above you. Beside it is a well, filled with dry rubble, and on the well a horn. As if in a dream, you lift it to your lips …

Only you can continue this meditation. Do you blow the horn? If so, wait and see what happens. Does a door open in the tower? If so, do you find the Fisher King? Is there something he needs from you? Or does the Damsel of the Well appear? If so, is she shrivelled and old as the well, or is she beautiful? How will you greet her and what does she give you in return?

# THE GRAIL
# CHRISTIANIZED

*And in the blast there smote along the hall*
*A beam of light seven times more clear than day:*
*And down the long beam stole the Holy Grail*
*All over covered with a luminous cloud.*
*And none might see who bare it, and it past.*[4]

In his *Story of the Grail*, Chrétien de Troyes does not tell us what the Grail is. But he does indicate that it is holy when he says that it contains a consecrated wafer which is enough to support the life of the Fisher King's father. However, because he died before completing the story, the mystery has never been resolved and the meaning of the Grail has never been explained.

After him several authors attempted to write a continuation of the legend. With each retelling, it became more strongly linked with Christ until, in 1200, Robert de Boron wrote his *Joseph of Arimathea*, based on the figure from the Bible.

# Joseph of Arimathea

Joseph was born at Arimathea, a Judean city, and was a wealthy and influential man in first-century Palestine. He is thought to have been a senator, perhaps a member of the Sanhedrin, the supreme council of the Jews. He was a secret disciple of Jesus because he was afraid of his position being compromised. However, after Jesus's crucifixion he asked Pontius Pilate to let him have the body of Christ. Permission being granted, he took the body to a tomb, hewed out of rock, that he had prepared for himself. His friend Nicodemus went with him and provided a quantity of spices for preparing the body, which they wrapped in linen and herbs. They then rolled a large stone over the entrance.

# The Cup of Christ

Robert de Boron takes the story of Joseph of Arimathea and links it with the story of the Grail to form a strongly Christianized version. At the same time he defines the Grail, making it both a physical and a spiritual object. He says that at the same time as Joseph of Arimathea acquired the body of Jesus, he also acquired the Cup of the Last Supper. This he uses to catch blood flowing from the body of Jesus. Afterwards he hides the cup in his house. Later, he is thrown into prison for his faith, but while he is languishing there, Christ appears to him and gives him the same cup, teaching him some holy words 'which are rightly called the secret of the Grail'.[5] Joseph is miraculously sustained by food provided by the chalice, now identified as the Holy Grail, until he is finally released from prison.

The story then becomes very involved. Joseph gathers up his family, including his sister and her husband Brons, and takes them travelling. At one stage they almost die of hunger, but magically a fish caught by Brons is converted by the Grail into enough food for the entire company. After this, Brons becomes known as the Rich

Fisher and is instructed by an angel to go west and await the arrival of his grandson, who will eventually receive the chalice as well as the secret words, so that he can understand its meaning.

This tale, although muddled and confusing, contains important new elements of the story. Firstly it links the Holy Grail with Christ through Joseph of Arimathea; secondly it attempts to explain the title of the Fisher King (at the same time suggesting an identification with Bran); and thirdly it seems to be concerned with some secret or mystery teachings concerning Christ.

# The Queste del Saint Graal

De Boron's *Joseph of Arimathea* paved the way for the vast Christian text known as the *Prose Lancelot* or the *Vulgate Cycle*. This was the text on which Malory later based his famous version of the legends of King Arthur. The *Vulgate Cycle* is an anonymous compilation of Arthurian stories written in French in the early 1200s. Although ascribed to someone called Walter Map, it is considered too extensive to be the work of one man and is now thought to have been written by a group of Cistercian monks. Certainly it reflects the teachings of their founder St Bernard of Clairvaux, who had a strong belief in the doctrine of grace and the mystical union of the soul with God.

The Cycle relates the entire story of King Arthur and his Knights leading up to the quest of the Grail. It also introduces, by a stroke of genius, the character of Galahad into the Arthurian legends. But in order to do so, it had to break the chivalric rules concerning adultery and chastity. The story is a curious one and concerns Lancelot's meeting with the Grail Maiden.

# Lancelot and the Maiden of the Grail

Lancelot comes upon the Castle of King Pelles (in some versions merged with King Pellam – see below). Here he meets the Grail Maiden, Elaine. With the connivance of her father, a powerful enchantress called Dame Brisen magically causes Elaine to take on the likeness of Queen Guinevere. In this way Lancelot is tricked into sleeping with her. The next morning, according to Malory, the 'fair lady Elaine skipped out of her bed all naked, and kneeled down afore Sir Lancelot'. She begs him not to kill her for her deception because 'the noblest knight of all the world' is in her womb. Lancelot forgives her and kisses her 'for she was as fair a lady, and thereto lusty and young'. Thus, out of the forbidden adulterous love between Lancelot and Guinevere, Galahad, the purest knight of all, is conceived.

# Galahad comes to Arthur's Court

Having established the birth of Galahad, the true Grail hero, the *Vulgate Cycle* goes on to tell of his first appearance at Arthur's Court. The account begins with an old man (later identified as Merlin) bringing Galahad to the Round Table and leading him to the *Siege Perilous*, the Dangerous Seat that has been designated for the perfect knight. After taking this seat, Galahad further demonstrates his superiority by being the only knight able to draw a magic sword from a floating block of red marble. This initiatory ritual echoes that of Arthur pulling the sword from the stone. It indicates that the story is moving into a new dimension in which the perfect knight is required to possess spiritual qualities that outstrip the former courtly ones.

When all the knights have resumed their seats at the Round Table, a ferocious clap of thunder is heard, after which a shaft of dazzlingly bright sunlight enters and illuminates the entire hall. Everyone present is struck dumb and remains in this state for a long time until the Holy Grail appears, covered with a cloth of white samite but not carried by any human hand. Immediately the palace is filled with a fragrance 'as though all the spices of the earth had been spilled abroad'. But this vision is tantalizingly incomplete because the Grail remains covered. After the Grail has disappeared and the power of speech has returned to the knights, Gawain pledges himself to go on the quest of the Grail, and the flower of Arthur's knights follow suit.

The ladies of the court wish to accompany them but an old hermit enters the hall and tells them that no man can take a woman with him on the quest for it is 'no search for earthly things but a seeking out of the mysteries and hidden sweets of Our Lord'.[6] Then Arthur, realizing this will mean the breaking up of the Fellowship of the Round Table, mourns the loss of his fair company. There follow the accounts of individual quests of the Grail in which the ultimate hero is now Galahad rather than Perceval. (For these see Chapter 4.)

# The Lance of Longinus

With the elaboration of the Arthurian Romances, not only was the Grail turned into the Cup of Christ, the blood-dripping spear was also Christianized. It was turned into the lance of Longinus, the Roman centurion who pierced Christ's side while he was on the Cross. Because the Cup of the Last Supper was also used by Joseph of Arimathea to catch the blood and water that issued from Christ's side, the connection between the two symbols – which the Celts had recognized – was cleverly preserved. Added to that, in order to make it sit happily in the Arthurian tradition, the lance was also linked with the one used by Sir Balin to deal the *Dolorous Stroke*.

# The Dolorous Stroke

This extraordinary story tells how Balin sets out on a quest and encounters Garlon, King Pellam's brother, who is said to be both black-faced and invisible. Because of his invisibility he can pick off other knights undetected. In this way he slays Balin's companion. Angrily, Balin rides on to the Castle of Carbonek (the Grail Castle), where he avenges his friend by killing Garlon with a well-aimed swipe of his sword. King Pellam immediately turns on Balin to avenge his brother. Balin breaks his sword in trying to defend himself and runs through the castle from chamber to chamber looking for a weapon, with King Pellam hard on his heels.

At last Balin comes into a rich chamber containing a bed and a gold table on silver legs. On this table is a 'marvellous spear strangely wrought'. Without pausing for thought, he snatches up the spear and strikes King Pellam with it, whereupon the King swoons and the castle roof and walls fall down. Balin and the Pellam lie under the rubble for three days until Merlin comes and rescues them. But Pellam continues to languish from his wound, waiting for Galahad's achievement of the Grail quest to restore his health.

# Joseph of Arimathea comes to Glastonbury

In some of the later Grail accounts, the Grail King is identified with Joseph of Arimathea. Because of the Grail stories, Joseph became very important and there is an apocryphal tradition concerning him which says he was the uncle of the Virgin Mary and therefore a relative of Jesus. This same legend goes on to tell how after the Crucifixion Joseph travelled to Gaul on a preaching mission, accompanied by a band of Christians who included the Apostle Philip, Lazarus and Mary Magdalene. They stopped off at the south of France, where Mary Magdalene disembarked with some of the

company, while the others kept travelling north until they reached England. Their boat ran aground at the Glastonbury marshes so they got out and climbed a hill in order to see the lie of the land.

Legend says that Joseph then thrust his staff (grown from Christ's Crown of Thorns) into the ground, declaring that they were all weary, whereupon it is said to have miraculously taken root and budded. After this, Joseph met with the ruler of Britain, Ariviragus, and was granted twelve hides of land at Glastonbury in order to establish the first monastery in Britain. His early wattle church was dedicated to the Virgin Mary but was unfortunately burned down in 1184. A few years later, however, with the supposed finding of Arthur's tomb, Glastonbury became such a great place of pilgrimage and attracted such revenue that the monks could afford to build the great abbey – the ruins of which still exist there.

By this time, owing to his founding of the first Christian Church, Joseph of Arimathea had become a saint and acquired cult status. Meanwhile a strong belief had arisen around him which said that he had brought the Chalice, or Cup of Christ, with him and that it was buried somewhere at Glastonbury.

## application

### A pilgrimage to Glastonbury

It is helpful for the Grail questor to visit some of the holy sites connected with the Grail legend. This is because he or she will encounter the energies of others on the quest. It will also involve the questor at a physical as well as a spiritual level in the search for the Grail. Glastonbury is a place highly charged with spiritual energy. Whether you believe the Grail can be found there or not, going to Glastonbury will be an important and instructive pilgrimage. The following visualization is a preparation for your visit, but can also be used by those who are unable to get there physically.

# Visualization

You begin your pilgrimage at the ancient Abbey, the place where Joseph of Arimathea built his church. Entering the ruins, you walk among half-rubbled walls, past arches and tall windows, through the long 'Galilee' to reach the Lady Chapel at the far end. Look up at the three perpendicular windows above you. This is where the first wattle church stood, dedicated to the Virgin Mary. There is peace here and great stillness. Ponder her wisdom.

Below the chapel is the crypt, dedicated to Joseph of Arimathea. This was once a dark and secret place with a mysterious well in a far dark corner. Imagine it as it once was and ponder the secret words that Joseph received from Jesus.

When you are ready make your way down the nave and through the tall broken archway into the choir. Go towards the high altar and stop at the grave of Arthur and Guinevere. Here were unearthed the bones of a giant of a man and the bones of a woman with a plaited lock of blonde hair. Yet tradition says Arthur has no grave and will come again. Even if this was not the grave of Arthur, stop and remember him. His court was worthy of the Grail, his knights worthy of its quest. He is still a power in the land.

Outside the Abbey you will find the Glastonbury Thorn, which took root from the staff of Joseph of Arimathea. This is grown from a slip of the first thorn tree which was cut down by a zealous Puritan. It still flowers out of season.

There are many ways from the Abbey to the Tor, which is where you are next headed. The route along Dod Lane is green and pretty and will take you straight to that extraordinary landmark. As you climb you see above you the ruins of St Michael's chapel, and the landscape spreading out below. Others are climbing with you, all believing in the spiritual presence there. You reach the top and sit and rest near the ruins looking out over the flat lands

*Joseph of Arimathea among the Rocks of Albion*, William Blake

around you. You might like to think about the power and beauty of the land, how it was once a lake, perhaps the mystical lake over which the dark barge sailed taking the dying Arthur to be healed. Three mysterious queens took him and he disappeared with them into the haze above the water.

When you are ready, descend the Tor and make your way to Chalice Well at the foot of Chalice Hill. You reach it through the beautiful and peaceful Chalice Gardens. The well is fed by a spring from which 25,000 gallons of pure water flow daily. The water is believed to have healing powers. Nearby is the White Spring. This also has healing powers. Drink from it. You are drinking the *Elixir Vitae*, the Waters of Life. Now go back and look deep into the waters of the Chalice Well. Is this where the Grail is hidden?

# 4  GRAIL QUESTS

The quest of the Grail was no ordinary one. Knights who had been used to their prowess and chivalry being tested were unprepared for the nature of such a quest. It went beyond bravery and skills in arms, beyond magic and beyond the psychological, and entered the realm of the spiritual. Of some 150 knights who set out on the quest, only five knights and one woman are reported to have come anywhere near to achieving it. There are also differing accounts of their quests which report varying degrees of success. Their individual experiences are detailed below. Some of the accounts are complex, so you may like to pick one or two for reading now and come back later to the others. Or you may like to read them all quickly and then return to the ones that you wish to work with. This chapter is intended to repay deeper study over a period of time.

# Gawain

Gawain is one of the original knights from the Celtic stories of
Arthur. His Welsh name is Gwalchmai, which means Hawk of May.
He was Arthur's nephew and champion and, in fact, would have
been next in line to Arthur's throne according to the Celtic system of
succession. In the earliest stories of the Grail quest his adventures
intertwine with those of Perceval, and some scholars think he may
have been the original Grail hero. But by the time Malory wrote his
version of the Grail story, Gawain had been superseded as chief
knight of the realm, first by Lancelot and then by Galahad.

# Gawain's quest

At the beginning of Malory's account, Gawain is weary, having set
out a long time before and as yet found no meaningful adventure.
He meets up with Sir Ector and they ride together until they come to
a derelict chapel. They enter to pray and then fall asleep. Gawain
has a dream in which he sees 150 bulls. All of them are black except
for three which are white, and one of these bears a black spot. Sir
Ector also has a strange dream. When they both awake a mysterious
hand and forearm, covered in red samite and holding a brightly
burning candle, appears and passes in front of them entering the
chapel and then vanishing. A voice tells them that they are both
lacking in faith and will not achieve the *Sangrail*.

They decide to go to Nacien the hermit for an explanation. On their
way Gawain jousts with a knight and kills him. He discovers, too
late, that he was Sir Uwain who was also on the quest of the Grail.
Nacien the hermit explains Gawain's dream which means that only
three knights are worthy of the quest. Two, Perceval and Galahad
are pure, while the third, Bors, is chaste, having only slept with a
woman once. The candle symbolizes the Holy Ghost.

After this, Gawain meets Sir Galahad, who smites him so hard that
his sword goes through his helmet and into his head. Then Galahad

disappears. Gawain, realizing that this stroke has been dealt him because he tried to pull the sword from the red marble slab, decides to stop seeking the Grail.

In this account Galahad appears like an avenging angel. He has not only superseded Gawain in pulling out the magic sword, but will also succeed in the quest where Gawain fails. However, three earlier accounts give Gawain better success. One is the first continuation of Chrétien de Troyes's original story, written by Gautier de Danans.

In this version Gawain stops to pray in a chapel and sees a great black hand appear and put out the altar light. He later arrives at the Grail Castle and goes into a room which contains the body of a knight holding a Cross and a Broken Sword. He dines that night with the Fisher King and sees the Grail procession. He is given the Broken Sword and asked to restore it (rather like Perceval in other accounts), but his failure to do so renders him unfit for the quest. He manages, however, to ask the meaning of the lance and is told it is the one which pierced Christ's side on the Cross. He falls asleep and awakes on the seashore surrounded by flowering countryside that has magically recovered because he learned the answer to one question. More would have been achieved if he could have asked about the Grail itself.

The motif of the sword is echoed in another account in the French text called the *Perlesvaus*. Here Gawain is only allowed to enter the Grail Castle once he has obtained the sword that beheaded St John the Baptist, which bleeds every day at noon. He finds the sword and witnesses the Grail procession, in which the shape of a child appears in the centre of the Grail. Three drops of blood drip onto the table in front of him and he becomes captivated by the sight and unable to speak. After this he sees the Grail high in the air and above it Christ nailed to the Cross with a spear in his side. He is so moved by this sight that, like Perceval, he fails to ask the question that would heal the land. He is then transported to the Castle with a magic chessboard (see Chapter 7).

In this story the motifs of the broken sword, the magic game of chess and the episode of the three drops of blood, are so similar to the adventures of Perceval, that it seems the two heroes were at one time interchangeable. As if to confirm this, there is one version in

which Gawain does succeed in the quest. This is in *Diu Crone* (The Crown) by Heinrich von dem Tulin. He tells how Gawain and Lancelot witness the Grail procession together, but Lancelot falls asleep so it is left to Gawain to ask the correct questions about the Grail. He does so and at once all those present, both the living and the dead, are released from their enchantments.

# Lancelot's quest

Lancelot initially sets out on the quest with Perceval. They meet Galahad, who is disguised, and each jousts with him. Galahad gets the better of them and then rides away so quickly that they are unable to catch up with him. After this Lancelot goes on alone until he comes to a crossroads at the edge of the Waste Land. Beside it is a derelict chapel, but inside the chapel Lancelot can see a rich altar with a six-branched silver candlestick on it which gives out a bright light. Lancelot finds he is unable to enter the chapel and instead falls asleep on his shield outside.

Lancelot then sees in a visionary dream a sick knight lying in a litter mourning for the presence of the holy vessel that will heal him. Then the Holy Grail appears and the knight sits up and kisses it and is immediately healed. The Grail then passes into the chapel. Lancelot is powerless to move. When he finally awakes he finds his helmet and sword have gone and he hears a voice that tells him he is harder than stone, more bitter than wood and more naked than the leaf of the fig tree.

He travels to a hermitage and is told by the hermit that his sin with Guinevere has prevented his achieving the Grail. He repents and travels on until he comes to the sea. He is told in a dream to enter a ship. The ship magically appears and he boards it to find a dead woman lying on a bed with a letter in her hand. (This is Dindrane, Perceval's sister – see page 36.) Galahad joins him on the ship and they spend half a year in each other's company meeting with adventures on various islands until Galahad is summoned by a White Knight to leave the ship.

Eventually Lancelot finds the Grail Castle and has to brave a pair of fierce lions by means of faith rather than prowess. Inside he finds the Grail Chamber but is unable to enter. He sees through the doorway the Holy Vessel covered with red samite, as well as a host of angels and a priest saying mass. The priest lifts up the body of a man as if it were the Host. Without thinking, Lancelot rushes forward to help him with the body, but feels as if he has met a wall of fire, and swoons. He is carried out of the chamber. Next day he is found as if dead and carried to a bed where he lies unable to open his eyes for twenty-four days. After recovering he is told that he is in the Castle of Carbonek. The Fisher King treats him with great respect. However, he is told that he has achieved as much of the *Sangrail* as is possible for him, and so he returns to Arthur's court.

# Bors's Quest

Sir Bors sets off on the quest and meets Nacien the hermit riding on an ass. He receives instruction from the hermit, who clothes him in a red gown. Bors determines to eat nothing but bread and water until he has achieved the quest. He rides on and comes to a parting of two ways. There he sees a naked man on horseback being beaten with thorns by two knights. The man looks up and Bors realizes with horror that it is his brother Sir Lionel. At the same time he hears the cries of a beautiful maiden who is being carried off by a knight on horseback in the other direction. Bors is torn between his duty to his brother and his oath to defend all women who call upon him. He decides to rescue the maiden and chases after her abductor, overcoming him and killing him. He then escorts her back to her castle.

Later he comes to a castle with a high tower. There he is made welcome by the Lady and her twelve women companions and offered rich food. However, he will eat only bread and water because of his vow. Then the Lady asks him to sleep with her. When he refuses, she says that if he will not love her, she and her maidens will all ascend the tower and jump off. Sir Bors is again in a

dilemma but sticks to his decision, whereupon they all jump. When they immediately disappear with much shrieking, Bors realizes that he was being tempted by an illusion.

After this he rides on and comes upon his brother, who has managed to escape from his oppressors. However, Lionel is so angry with Bors for not rescuing him that he threatens to kill him. Bors will not fight his brother and a hermit intervenes and is killed in his place. Lionel again attempts to kill Bors, but Bors draws his sword. Then a voice warns him not to kill his brother and a fiery cloud appears and burns both their shields. They both fall down in a swoon. When they recover, Lionel begs Bors to forgive him, which he does gladly, before riding away.

Bors then comes to the sea and boards a ship, on which he finds Perceval. Galahad joins them and Bors becomes one of the company of successful knights who achieve the Grail and also travel to the Holy City of Sarras. Bors eventually returns to Arthur's court to tell of the quest.

# Dindrane's quest

Dindrane is Perceval's sister who becomes part of the Grail company on the magic ship. Although she does not achieve the Grail, she fails for the noblest of reasons.

Dindrane appears in *Perlesvaus* as a mysterious but saintly figure, then again in Malory. She guides Sir Galahad to the magic ship and boards it with him. They find Perceval and Bors already on it. She then acts as guide to all three of them and instructs them to board another ship. Then she reveals to Perceval that she is his sister. She shows them the strange objects on the ship, a rich bed, a crown and a sword, and says that only Galahad is worthy to draw the sword. She then gives them explanations for the strange objects. The sword is the sword of David, and the bed is the Tree of Life, linked with Adam and Eve and also with King Solomon. She then makes new girdles, or hangings, for the sword using her own hair.

The four of them come to a castle and are constrained to go in because the custom of the castle forbids any virgin to pass without giving a dish of her blood. This is because the lady of the castle has been languishing from leprosy for many years and has been told that this is how she will be healed. Dindrane willingly gives her blood and dies as a result, although the lady of the castle is healed. In this strange feminine mirroring of the Fisher King's malady, Dindrane's blood caught in the silver dish becomes the equivalent of the Grail and her sacrificial death is like that of Galahad when he achieves the Grail.

Dindrane makes a final request. Before she dies she asks that her body be put in a barge covered in black silk and left to the mercy of the sea. She prophesies that she will arrive at the City of Sarras (see below) before the other three and asks them to bury her there. Perceval writes an account of their strange adventures and puts it in her right hand. This is how she is found by Lancelot when he himself boards a boat before being joined by Galahad. This is a curious inversion of the tale of the Fair Maid of Astolat (the Lady of Shalott), who died for love of Lancelot and was put in a barge covered in black samite that floated down to Camelot.

Although Dindrane does not achieve the Grail, there is a compelling episode in *Perlesvaus* in which she has a foretaste of it. This is when, all alone, she braves the horrible Perilous Cemetery, which is haunted by the ghosts of unrepentant Black Knights. She passes through it and eventually reaches the chapel in the middle, finding it filled with light. There she has a vision of the Virgin Mary and sees a holy cloth on the chapel altar. It rises up in the air but she begs to be allowed to have some of the cloth, which she knows is the shroud that was used to wrap the body of Christ. The cloth descends to the altar and she is given a portion of it. This strange story in which Dindrane has to go alone and cannot be accompanied by her brother, suggests it is connected with the Feminine Mysteries, or ancient secret religious practices.

# Perceval's quest

In the early stories Perceval is presented as a type of Perfect Fool. His naivety and innocence are part of what fits him for the role of hero. He acquires prowess and courtliness as he journeys towards his destiny. Although his story breaks off or is unconvincingly wrapped up in the two earliest versions, in some continuations he achieves the Grail quest a second time, asks the Question and brings about the healing of the Fisher King. There are also accounts of his replacing the Fisher King as the keeper of the Grail and taking Blancheflor as his wife.

In the *Perlesvaus*, Perceval has his own adventures alone on board a magical ship which takes him to several mysterious islands, one of which contains a community of thirty-three priestly men who seem like an inner circle of initiates (see Chapter 6). In this version he becomes the Grail King and returns to rule an Elysian Island of Plenty.

In the later versions found in the *Vulgate Cycle* and in Malory, Perceval is superseded by Galahad but becomes linked with him and Sir Bors when all three travel on the magical Ship of Solomon in the final stages of the Grail quest. Although he outlives Galahad by just over a year, dying in a hermitage in Sarras, in this account he is really only a facet of Galahad.

# Galahad's quest

Although Galahad becomes the final Grail knight, he is hardly a human figure at all. He appears like an initiating angel to joust with Lancelot, Bors and Perceval when they are embarked on the Grail quest. After each occasion he miraculously disappears. He also at this time rides incognito carrying a white shield bearing a red cross that has been made by the blood of Joseph of Arimathea, issuing from his nose. Galahad is said to be a direct descendant of Joseph of Arimathea, as is his father, Lancelot.

There are two accounts of Galahad sailing on magic ships. In one he accompanies his father, and in this he can be seen as relating to or identifying with him. In fact it could be argued that Lancelot achieves the Grail through his son. Conversely, Galahad's spiritual achievement can also be seen as emmanating from his father's physical prowess and courtliness. Certainly the flawed man and the spiritual one are linked.

When he boards the second ship Galahad becomes the leader of the trio of men who achieve the Grail together. Dindrane, who sails with them, is a type of the feminine spirit of wisdom who guides them. After splitting up and reuniting, the three knights eventually arrive at the Castle of Carbonek together and are presented with the Broken Sword. Galahad is the only one who can mend it but he then presents it to Bors.

Just before they see the Grail procession the Maimed King is carried in on 'a bed of tree', with a gold crown on his head. The Grail procession is led by a man who is said to be Joseph, the first Christian bishop who was succoured in the spiritual palace in the city of Sarras. Angels follow him bearing candles, a towel and a spear that bleeds into a box. According to Malory, the bishop lifts up a wafer resembling bread, whereupon the figure of a child with a face as bright as fire 'smote himself into the bread'.

The bread is returned to the holy vessel and changes into the bleeding body of Christ, who mystically gives himself as the Host to the three knights. They all partake of the Grail but it is Galahad who anoints the Maimed King with blood that has dripped from the lance, after which he is healed. The three knights are told by Christ to take the holy vessel to Sarras in order to experience its powers more fully.

This they do, but when they arrive they are immediately imprisoned by the King and, like Joseph of Arimathea, are kept alive only by the sustenance of the Grail. After a year, however, the King falls ill and asks their forgiveness. The King then dies and the people of Sarras are instructed by a disembodied voice to choose Galahad as his successor. After a year Galahad receives a mystical mass from Joseph of Arimathea and dies, whereupon he is carried up to Heaven by angels along with the Grail and the Holy Lance. In this

enactment of the Resurrection, Galahad is clearly shown to be a type of Christ, the Grail having been demonstrated as the Chalice of the Mass, containing the body as well as the blood of Christ.

*The Grail Heroes*

# ApplICATION

As is evident from the accounts given above, the quests are all different, each being related to the deeds and character of the particular questor. It is important to remember that the quest is an individual one. This is why the road is often lonely. The knights were pitted against themselves in their efforts to reach the highest goal possible. Their only guides were the solitary hermits they encountered in the forests. There was no Church or ecclesiastical hierarchy to guide them because the path was not a general one.

You may like to choose one of the quests for meditation. They are complicated but will repay study. If you have difficulty choosing, these are the main characteristics of the different questors:

**Gawain**

The most ancient and Celtic of the questors, Gawain was the first to jump up and offer to go on the quest. He is spontaneous but sometimes lacks stamina. He is one of the most gentle and courteous of Arthur's knights. He is especially sensitive to the needs of women and is also merciful to vanquished enemies. He

is one of the finest champions of Arthur's court. Although in some tales he has the wit to give up the quest when he realizes it is not for him, in others he wins through like Perceval.

## Lancelot

This hero has reached the highest point possible in terms of prowess and skill in arms. His courtliness is also legendary. The trouble is that this extends to a love for Guinevere which goes beyond the bounds of chivalry into adultery. He has therefore betrayed his king and curbed his own spiritual potential. He is the flawed hero.

Nevertheless he has two options. He can repent and give up his adulterous love, in which case he is not too late to achieve the full experience of the Grail, or he can continue his quest and accept a limited mystical experience. In the end he opts for the limited experience. Nevertheless just by attempting the quest he encounters his unknown son and also achieves some experience of the Grail. However, this is almost too much for him and he takes a long time to recover from it. His quest can be seen therefore as both encouraging and cautionary.

## Perceval

Considered the original Grail hero, Perceval is also naïve and plays the part of the Fool, especially at the outset of his career. Nevertheless his initial innocence gives him special insight into the spiritual side of life. He is enthusiastic, like Gawain, but also has an Otherworldly nobility, especially towards the end of his quest. In some accounts he not only achieves the Grail, but becomes the Grail King, ruling over the restored land, together with his wife and two sons. He is able to combine spirituality, love and family life.

## Bors

Bors is in some ways the least flamboyant and most down-to-earth of the questors. However, when he is preparing for his quest he does receive some strong visionary dreams. He is very

determined. He finds decisions difficult but, when he has made up his mind, he sticks to it. He manages to resist the Lady's advances in the castle and he does his best in the impossible situation where he has to choose between helping his brother or the abducted maiden. He demonstrates great nobility when his brother nearly kills him and, as a result, is rescued by supernatural forces.

He is privileged to be part of the final trio accompanying Galahad on the last stages of the journey. Galahad considers him worthy of the mended sword. But, unlike Galahad, Bors is not so spiritual that he wishes to expire after achieving the Grail. He returns to Arthur's court to tell the story and resume a normal life.

## Dindrane

Dindrane's experience is the least clear-cut. In some ways she does not really go on her own journey. She accompanies the three heroes on the final stages of their quest but gives up her life on the way. It seems as if she has already experienced the Grail and is closely involved with it in ways that the others have yet to discover. She has the gift of foreknowledge, which suggests that she is an Otherworldly figure. In meditation, she can be sought as a guide alongside any of the other questors. She also represents an inner experience of the Grail and of the feminine Mysteries which lie deeper than words. She is a very powerful helper on the quest.

## Galahad

Galahad is also an Otherworldly figure. He is too perfect to be human. Born solely for the Grail quest, he has inherited the prowess of his father but goes beyond him in spiritual attainment. He demonstrates a balance of masculine and feminine energies. In his warrior aspect he is a challenger, but he is also a healer, having healed the Fisher King.

In your strivings on your quest, take heart and encouragement from the great figures who have gone before you. Meet them in your meditations and learn from their experiences.

# THE GNOSTIC GRAIL

*Passionate, with longing in my eyes,*
*Searching wide, and seeking nights and days,*
*Lo! I beheld the Truthful One, the Wise,*
*Here in mine own house to fill my gaze.*[7]

In Chapter 4 we saw how, according to legend, Joseph of Arimathea travelled to England with the Holy Grail. He was accompanied by a band of Christian believers, among whom was Mary Magdalene. The company split into two groups, some staying behind in France, while Joseph and the others carried on to England. This has given rise to speculation that the Grail may have been buried at Glastonbury, possibly in or near the Chalice Well.

An alternative theory claims that the Grail stayed behind in France with Mary Magdalene. This provocative theory involves the cult of the Magdalene, as well as that of the Black Madonna, and not least the heretical faith of the *Cathars*, who lived in the Languedoc area in the south of France.

# MARY MAGDALENE

Mary Magdalene is known from the gospel stories as the woman from whom Jesus cast out seven devils and who thereafter became his close companion and follower. She is also often identified with the woman who anointed his feet with costly nard, or perfume, and wiped them with her hair. She was also present at the Crucifixion and she was the first person to see the risen Christ. Despite this honour, a strong tradition has grown up around her suggesting that she was a prostitute who was reformed by her contact with Christ, but this is not substantiated by the Bible.

Ancient texts have recently come to light, however, which seem to show that this portrayal of Mary Magdalene as a fallen woman is inaccurate. There is now a belief that the casting out of the seven devils may refer to an initiation ceremony that she had undergone as part of an Egyptian Mystery Religion, the Cult of Isis (see page 51), to which she may have belonged. There has also been a suggestion that she came from a wealthy family and even that she was the consort or wife of Jesus. These incredible theories have come from perusal of the ancient texts known as the *Nag Hammadi Scrolls*.

# The Nag Hammadi Scrolls

In 1945 an Egyptian peasant was digging for *sabakh*, the fertile soil created by the latrines of the early hermits who had lived in caves near the village of Nag Hammadi in Upper Egypt. Suddenly he came upon a large jar made of red earthenware. He smashed it and found inside fifty-two papyrus scrolls bound in leather. He took them home, where his mother burned some of them in the oven. Fortunately the rest were taken to the local priest and were spotted by a local historian, who alerted an expert in Cairo. Finally, after much difficulty and in-fighting amongst experts and governments, the texts were translated and have now become known to the general public.

The papyri are dated at 350–400 CE and are Coptic translations of even earlier Greek texts. The date of the earlier texts is uncertain; many of them are contemporary with the gospels, but some may be pre-Christian. The whole collection includes texts such as the *Gospel of Thomas*, the *Gospel of Philip*, the *Secret Gospel of John*, the *Gospel of Truth*, and the *Gospel to the Egyptians* (also called 'The Sacred Book of the Great Invisible Spirit'), as well as poems, myths, and instruction for the practice of Mystery religions. The existence of some of these texts was already known from the writings of Bishop Irenaeus, who was condemning heresies as early as the second century CE.

These gospels, denounced as heretical by the growing orthodoxy of the Early Church Fathers, contain sayings of Jesus which are either different from those in the biblical gospels, or which can be viewed differently because of the new context in which they are placed. In terms of the quest for the Holy Grail, there are two particularly radical conclusions that can be drawn from this material.

The first is the importance of Mary Magdalene, who is named as the 'companion' or 'partner' of Jesus, and who was sufficiently intimate with Jesus for him to kiss her on the mouth:

> ... *the companion of the [Saviour is] Mary Magdalene. [But Christ loved] her more than [all] the disciples and used to kiss her [often] on her [mouth]. The rest of [the disciples were offended by it...] They said to him, 'Why do you love her more than all of us?' The Saviour answered and said to them, 'Why do I not love you as [I love] her?'* [8]

This quote is from the *Gospel of Philip*, which also relates the rivalry that came about between Mary Magdalene and Peter. Peter did not believe that women were worthy to be full followers of Christ and therefore disputed Mary's claim to having been taught special knowledge or *gnosis*, by Jesus. But in the *Dialogue of the Saviour* she is praised as a visionary who has been selected by Christ for special teaching. She is described as the 'woman who knew the All'.

Several sayings to this effect among the Nag Hammadi texts link with an earlier scroll, one of four, discovered in Egypt in 1896. This

was the *Gospel of Mary* (Magdalene). It opens with the reaction of the disciples after Jesus's death. They are terrified for their own lives but Mary Magdalene reassures them of Christ's continual presence. The fact that she has already seen him accords with the account given in St Mark's Gospel, but in this gospel she tells them she has received further teaching from him in a vision. When the disciples dispute this she weeps and says to Peter:

> '*My brother Peter, what do you think? Do you think that I thought this up myself in my heart? Do you think I am lying about the Saviour?' Levi answered and said to Peter, 'Peter, you have always been hot-tempered...If the Saviour made her worthy, who are you to reject her?*' [9]

This is the beginning of a rift between Peter and Mary which became a serious doctrinal schism in the early Church. Mary claims to have seen the risen Christ and received teachings from him in a vision received 'through the mind'. She is not talking about a physically risen Christ, but a spiritual presence.

# A spiritual resurrection

This brings us to the second great revelation of these so-called *Gnostic Gospels*. They state that not only Mary but also some of the disciples received secret teachings from Jesus to the effect that the idea of the resurrection of the body was a crude misunderstanding of spiritual truth. This rejection of the bodily resurrection of Christ was linked to the concept of *dualism*, the split between the spiritual and the material, which formed the core belief of the great heresy called *Gnosticism*, espoused by a group of early Christians. By the time of the Crusades this heresy was still strongly active and its main adherents were known as the Cathars.

# The Cathars

The Cathars were also sometimes called the *Albigensians* because they lived near the town of Albi in the Languedoc area of southern France. They were attracted to this area because it was known for its religious tolerance, being independent from France at the time. New intellectual and philosophical ideas were able to flourish there, and it was also the home of the new Courtly Love poetry of the troubadours.

Although the Cathars considered themselves Christians, they claimed to have a special understanding of Christianity. They followed the secret teachings of Jesus which, they said, were found in mystical experience, just as Mary Magdalene described. They believed that whereas Jesus taught only in parables to the general mass of his followers, he taught a secret higher knowledge to his disciples which they passed on only to those who were ready to understand it.

There are accounts in several of the Gnostic Gospels of some of the disciples having mystical experiences. For example, in the *Apocryphon of John*, John recounts how he was in 'great grief' after the Crucifixion:

> Immediately...the [heavens were opened, and the whole] creation [which is] under heaven shone, and [the world] was shaken. [I was afraid, and I] saw in the light [a child] ...while I looked he became like an old man. And he [changed his] form again, becoming like a servant ...I saw ... a[n image] with multiple forms in the light ...[10]

In such accounts Jesus manifests himself not in bodily form but as a luminous presence or in a series of transformations. The Cathars believed that truth was revealed in this way and that such experience was open to anyone. They rejected the idea that Christians needed priestly intervention or instruction from the Church. In fact, they rejected Church-based Christianity, believing it had become corrupted and patriarchal.

Because Mary Magdalene was the first to receive direct experience of the secret teachings of Christ, she became a figurehead for the Gnostics. They also venerated the idea of the Divine Feminine, which they felt was lacking in orthodox Christianity. They prayed to both the Divine Father and the Divine Mother. Sometimes the Divine Mother was worshipped independently as 'the mystical, eternal Silence', and a secret mass was held in which the wine symbolized her blood.

The Cathars also identified the Divine Feminine with the Holy Spirit. There is evidence from the Gnostic Gospels that the Holy Spirit was at one time considered to be female. For example, in his *Gospel* Philip indignantly refutes the idea that Mary could have become pregnant by the Holy Spirit. He says: 'Some say that Mary conceived by the holy spirit: they are mistaken, they do not realize what they say. When did a female ever conceive by a female?'[11]

The Cathars also linked the Divine Feminine principle with the ancient Greek concept of *Sophia*, the female spirit of wisdom. The opening of John's Gospel was their credo. They believed Wisdom was 'the Word', who was 'in the beginning' and was 'with God'. She was also the Spirit who 'moved on the face of the waters' to effect the Creation. As such she was the feminine principle that lay behind the Creator God and was, some believed, more powerful.

All in all, the Cathars, in their reverence for the feminine, their disbelief in a physical resurrection and their belief in knowledge through spiritual revelation rather than doctrine, were considered dangerous heretics by the Roman Catholic Church. They were especially dangerous because their beliefs were popular and posed a real threat to orthodox Christianity.

# The Albigensian Crusade

In 1208 Pope Innocent III called for a huge army to fight against the heretical Cathars. Although they considered themselves fellow Christians, the Pope considered them as threatening as the Muslims. The Albigensian Crusade was treated in the same way as the other

Crusades, with knights being offered *indulgences*, or pardons, in return for their services. The area targeted was Languedoc and it was difficult for the crusading knights to distinguish orthodox Catholics from heretics because they were coexisting peacefully. The appalling command from the papal legate has become infamous. He said: 'Kill them all, God will recognize his own!' The result was a huge massacre of the population of southern France.

Last to fall was the great Cathar stronghold, the castle on the mountain at Montségur. This had been deliberately fortified for the protection of the heretics and was also said to hold the 'Cathar Treasure'. In 1243 Montségur was besieged by an army of ten thousand men, and finally fell. The site below it is famous for the rounding up and mass burning of more than two hundred devotees. It is know today as the 'Field of the Burned' .

After the fall of Montségur, the treasure was collected up, but much of it was found to have gone. Tradition has it that during the siege four of the *Parfaits*, or *Perfecti*, the leaders of the Cathar faith, had escaped by rope down the mountainside, taking the treasure with them. This treasure has excited much speculation. Many believe that the most important and holy item they possessed was the Holy Grail itself.

One theory as to how it might have come into their possession is that it was brought over by Mary Magdalene. A cult of the Magdalene grew up in that area of France, as is still evident from the number of churches dedicated to her. It seems feasible that if she took refuge there then the Cathars, who revered her, should become the possessors of her treasure.

# ARThURIAN LEGEND — a SECRET CODE?

At the time when the Cathars were flourishing, the Arthurian legends were becoming extremely popular. Although the Catholic Church was suspicious of these stories they tolerated them because they

inspired knights to join the Crusades. They were suspicious of them because, although Arthur purported to be Christian, his Celtic origins were everywhere apparent in the stories, not least in the number of Celtic hermits that abounded in independent chapels in the mysterious forests where the knights' prowess was tested. Moreover, these hermits were always urging the knights on in their solitary efforts at self-improvement, thus suggesting that salvation could be attained through personal effort. This ran counter to the Church's belief in salvation through faith and, in particular, to the importance of the Church's sacraments and the role of its priests.

The other worrying aspect of the Arthurian legends was their adherence to the ideal of Courtly Love. This strange phenomenon had suddenly arisen in the poetry of the troubadours who lived in the Languedoc. Many theories have been put forward for this extraordinary new idealism in which women were made into objects of worship and adoration. The chivalric code of the knights served this ideal and their highest task seemed to be the service of women.

One theory put forward for this sudden elevation of the feminine is that it was an encoded form of the secret Feminine Mysteries espoused by the heretical sects. Knights on crusade had come into contact with Eastern mysticism, especially that of the *Sufis*, the heretical sect of orthodox Islam. It is well known that the Sufis' erotic love poetry was a coded form of worship of the Divine Feminine principle, and the Courtly Love motif of troubadour poetry and Arthurian legend may have performed the same function.

# A home for the Grail

If this were the case then it would be entirely appropriate that the story of the Holy Grail should be linked to the Arthurian Cycle. Arthur's knights were already inspired to extremes of personal prowess by devotion to the Feminine, so for them to seek the Holy Grail, a symbol of the highest form of spirituality, seems a natural progression – especially if it represented the secret female aspect of the deity.

Also, some of the descriptions of the Grail given in the Arthurian stories are very suggestive of the mystical experiences of Christ described in the Gnostic Gospels. For example, the idea of a great light emanating from the Grail, or the form of a child in the Grail who then turns into a man, is reminiscent of the transformations reported by the Gnostic visionaries. Also in the Grail stories there is a report of Arthur himself seeing five different transformations of the Grail. This is in *Perlesvaus*, the anonymous French account of the Grail, which is arguably one of the most mystical. By contrast Malory seems determined to show the contents of the Grail as the transubstantiated body of Christ. His description is heavy-handed, almost as if he is trying to refute the suggestions made in previous accounts.

# The cult of Isis

If the Grail symbolizes the Feminine Mysteries espoused by the Cathars, and if they were sceptical of the bodily resurrection of Christ then, it has been argued, their beliefs might go back to pre-Christian goddess worship. The most obvious candidate for this would be Isis, the great Egyptian goddess who was also regarded as the female principle of Nature.

The central story enshrined in her religion was that of the death and resurrection of Osiris, her consort. After he was killed by his evil brother she restored him to life. His resurrection was ritualistic and connected with cyclical renewal, fertility and the changing seasons. It therefore represented a mystery, a hidden spiritual truth, rather than being an actual physical occurrence. This was akin to the way in which the Gnostics regarded the resurrection of Christ. Certainly at the time of Christ the cult of Isis was still very strong. It is thought that some of the rituals used by Christianity may have been taken from it. For example, baptism was used by adherents of Isis to symbolize the washing away of sins.

Isis, herself, being an Earth goddess, was symbolic of the rich black soil that lined the Nile. She was often portrayed as a black mother

holding a baby. This baby was Horus, son of her husband Osiris whom she brought back to life. Isis became the most prominent deity of Egypt, revered for her powers in connection with the resurrection of Osiris. She demonstrated the force of feminine love in conquering the death of the masculine.

Notre Dame de Clermont-Ferrand

# The Black Madonna

The image of Isis as the black mother goddess holding her baby is believed to have prefigured the statues of the Virgin Mary with the child Jesus. The extraordinary proliferation of Black Madonnas in the south of France supports this idea. It is well known that shrines to the Virgin Mary or to the saints were erected on ancient pagan sites and even that the names of the ancient deities were Christianized, so it is feasible to conjecture that a former pagan goddess cult in which a black goddess or Dark Mother was

venerated, might be transformed into a sanctuary for the worship of the Virgin and Child.

It is thought to be no accident that the Grail legends, the cult of the Magdalene and the cult of the Black Madonna all became prominent in the area of Languedoc at the same time. This elevation of the Feminine, especially in its dark and mysterious aspect, has been explained psychologically as a reaction to the suppression of the feminine principle in orthodox Christianity. The only image allowed by the Roman Church was the chaste image of the Virgin, who was elevated to such a height of perfection that she could not, like the pagan representations of the Goddess, embody dual aspects of personality.

In the figure of the Virgin Mary, therefore, the negative or dark side of the feminine deity was split off. The Black Madonnas, by contrast, are thought to be manifestations of the neglected negative aspect of the Divine Feminine. It was, of course, the dark side of the Feminine that contained the secret teachings, the hidden mysteries and the divine gnosis.

The connection between the Black Madonna and the Grail is shown in the legends by the appearance of the loathly damsel Cundrie, who is called the Black Woman in *Peredur*. Despite her horrific appearance, she is intimately connected with the mysteries of the Grail. Not only does she follow Perceval to Arthur's Court and influence him to attempt the quest a second time, she also guides him. In fact, he goes so far as to seek her out when embarking on the quest, as he realizes that only she can help him to attain his goal.

## APPLICATION

### Honouring the Dark Goddess

*I am black, but beautiful*
*O ye daughters of Jerusalem*

Although banished, the Dark Goddess still has her place. She can even be found in the pages of the Old Testament's Song of

Solomon. The ancient understanding of her was as the container of opposites such as death and life, male and female, creation and destruction. The Celts had their triple goddess with three aspects: maiden, mother and crone. Other ancient religions also acknowledged and honoured the different sides of the feminine deity. Only the Christian religion split her in two, finding her dark face unacceptable. But still she returns, as the Black Madonna or, more dangerously, as an angry, destructive sorceress or witch.

The dark aspect of the Goddess symbolizes destruction, chaos, death. In Jungian terms, unintegrated with her bright side, she can become uncontrollable. Her wise worshippers of old knew how to honour her in all her guises and to preserve her unity. But for the last millennium there has been a widespread dishonouring of women and female powers. Today, at a psychological level, and also at a spiritual one, there is a dawning realization that in the dishonouring of women through fear of their dark side, something of crucial importance has been lost.

This is what the Goddess, be she Isis, Sophia or one of the other myriad ancient female deities, has said about herself in one of the Gnostic Gospels. Ponder on it. Allow her dark face as well as her bright one to give you wisdom, her counsel to give you insight. Then explore her nature further by composing your own poem or creative work in her honour.

> *For it is I who am the first: and the last.*
> *It is I who am the revered: and the despised.*
> *It is I who am the harlot: and the holy.*
> *It is I who am the wife: and the virgin.*
> *It is I who am the mother: and the daughter…*
> *It is I who am the barren: and who has many children.*
> *It is I who am the one whose marriage is magnificent:*
> *and who have not married.*
> *It is I who am the midwife: and she who does not give birth…*
> *It is I who am the bride: and the bridegroom…*
> *And may those who have not recognized me become acquainted*
> *with me.*[12]

# 6 THE TEMPLARS' GRAIL

*Flegetanis knew the starry script
could read in the heavens high
How the stars roll on their courses,
how they circle the silent sky
And the time when the wandering endeth
– and the life and the lot of men
He read in the stars, and strange secrets he saw.*[13]

## The Knights Templars

When the Albigensian Crusade was launched by the Roman Catholic Church (see Chapter 5), there was one group of knights who refused to take part. These were the Knights Templars. This intriguing secret order seems to have had a close affinity with the Cathars. Indeed there are some who believe that at the time of

The Seal of the Knights Templars

the great massacre of Cathars some members of the sect smuggled the Holy Grail out of Montségur and passed it to the Templars.

Certainly the Knights Templars have always been strongly linked with the Holy Grail. In fact, they have even been called the Keepers of the Grail. But who they were exactly, what their real purpose was, and where the extraordinary power they wielded at the time of the Crusades came from, are questions shrouded in mystery.

# Mysterious Origins

Around 1119, nine French noblemen led by a certain Hughes de Payens went to the King of Jerusalem and asked permission to form an order of Poor Knights, or warrior monks, whose function would be to serve in the Holy Land. Permission was granted and they were established in the Al-Aqsa Mosque on the site of the former Temple of Solomon (destroyed by the Romans in 68 CE). It was from this temple that they got their name.

Strangely, although their alleged purpose was to protect pilgrims, for nine years they did not increase their numbers but remained on the Temple site in Jerusalem. So it was not until 1128 that they were given official recognition at the Council of Troyes. It was also at this time that St Bernard of Clairvaux, founder of the Cistercian Order, wrote their Rule.

Being a monkish order the Templars had to adhere to the three vows of poverty, chastity and obedience. They were therefore not allowed to marry and no women were permitted to join the order. They wore white robes to which they later added the distinctive red cross *pattée* – a Celtic, or equal-armed, cross with splayed ends, which was also emblazoned on their shields.

# An influential force

After 1128 the Templars dramatically increased their numbers and, at the same time, started becoming extremely wealthy. Money was raised to fund their order and they also acquired lands and castles from the noblemen who joined them. Using their castles as strongholds, they became the bankers for the Crusades. They gained great respect and were even consulted by Kings. They were also granted privileges by the Pope, including tax exemption. In the end they obtained such financial and religious freedom that they became a law unto themselves.

# Free thinkers

The result of all this was that the Templars were able to enjoy independence of thought. They were not dominated by the orthodox teaching of the Roman Catholic Church, and at the same time they were exposed to the sophistication of Eastern philosophy. Many of them learned Arabic or employed Arabic secretaries and discovered that the 'infidels' were in many ways more learned and civilized than the Christians.

The freedom of exchange of information enjoyed by the Templars meant that they were able to bring back to the West important new ideas in medicine, masonry and architecture. They also investigated the mathematical, astronomical, philosophical and religious learning of the East. At the same time they amply fulfilled their stated

purpose. They were an extremely disciplined force of proud and brave warriors who were prepared to fight to the death to support the cause of the Crusades.

Although the Crusades began well, with the Christian armies initially capturing Jerusalem, their position gradually worsened over the years. While the enemy had been divided within itself between Muslim and Mongol forces, the Christians had enjoyed the advantage, but when the Muslims defeated the Mongols and were then joined by the Mamluks, the Christian cause became increasingly hopeless. After a long struggle Saladin, King of Egypt, captured Jerusalem in 1187 and the Templars were forced out of the city, moving their headquarters to Cyprus. The Crusades continued for another hundred years but after the siege of Acre in 1291 they were effectively over.

With the ending of the wars the purpose of the Templars was apparently gone, but they remained as an independent secret society, swearing allegiance to one another rather than to any king or country. Rumours grew up around them suggesting that they now had some other purpose, perhaps involving some kind of secret knowledge or information.

# Strange rituals

Although they had commanded such respect during the Crusades, it is easy to see why the Templars became discredited. Although it was not their fault, they were criticized for the loss of Jerusalem. They were also accused of collaborating with the enemy in order to protect their wealth. Much of this criticism came from fear and jealousy. Their wealth and independence must have made them seem very threatening. Rumours arose concerning strange rituals performed in their secret initiation ceremonies. These included worshipping cats, Satanic idols and mysterious heads, killing babies, eating the ashes of dead Templars and spitting on images of the Cross. They were also believed to be magicians, alchemists and occultists and, as such, were accused of practising witchcraft and supporting heretical beliefs.

# Persecution of the Templars

With the declared aim of purifying France of heresies – but probably because he needed money – Philip IV of France sent hundreds of his agents out on Friday 13 October and arrested the French Templars *en masse*, with no prior warning. These arrests were actually illegal but the Pope owed his position to Philip so had no choice but to side with him. With the Pope's support, other raids were made across Europe and the Templars were put on trial.

The charges laid against them hinged on their alleged denial of the Crucifixion. Under extreme torture, confessions were obtained that supported these charges as well as some of the strange rumours. For an order which had been highly respected as upholders of Christianity, these admissions were shocking. Even so, nothing could be proved conclusively against them and as a result no final verdict was ever reached. Nevertheless, as a result of Philip bullying the Pope, the entire order was officially dissolved in March 1312.

# The curse of the Templars

Two years later, the Grand Master of the Templars, Jacques de Molay, was sentenced to life imprisonment, having also confessed to iniquitous practices. But instead of accepting his sentence, at the last minute he retracted his confession saying that his only sin was that of lying under torture and admitting to 'the disgusting charges laid against the Order'. He declared that the Order was innocent, 'its purity and saintliness' beyond question. He ended by stating that because life was offered to him only 'at the price of infamy', it was not worth having.

Accordingly, Jacques de Molay was condemned to death and was burned alive along with Geoffrey de Charnay, the Preceptor of Normandy, outside the Cathedral of Notre Dame. Before he died, de

Molay cursed Philip of France and the Pope for their crimes against the Templars, calling for their reckoning within a year. Within the year both were dead.

# Treasures of the Templars

After their dissolution, the mystique of the Templars persisted, not least because of the disappearance of their treasure. If Philip IV was hoping to get his hands on it he was disappointed. After the trials surprisingly little of it was found, but this was given by the Pope to the Order of the Knights Hospitallers. So what had happened to the rest of it? Some believe that despite the suddenness of Philip's arrests, word had leaked out just in time for some of the Templars to set sail from the west coast of France, where their fleet was moored, and take their most important treasures elsewhere. Naturally, if it was in their keeping, their chief treasure would have been the Holy Grail itself.

The idea that the Templars were the guardians of the Grail has always been a strong one, not least because it is supported in two important Grail texts. These lie slightly outside the main Grail canon because they were not directly used by Malory. They are the anonymous French *Perlesvaus* and the German *Parzival*.

# The Templars as a mystical sect in Perlesvaus

This lively account, also called *The High History of the Grail*, contains such knowledgeable and detailed descriptions of battle that some have suggested it may have actually been written by a

Templar. It also contains two passages which seem to relate directly to the Templars.

One is when Perceval is taken by magic ship to an island where he comes across two masters and thirty-three men in white robes which bear red crosses. These would appear to be initiates of some sort and they are certainly wearing the Templar costume. They tell him about a quantity of heads sealed in lead, silver and gold, and more specifically, of the head of a king and a queen. These sealed heads strongly suggest both alchemy and the cult of the severed head, which goes back to the Celtic god Bran, but they are also linked with the secret rituals of the Templars. The second passage is when a priest is depicted as defiling the Cross by hitting it. This is similar to the confessions extracted from the Templars under torture.

It also reflects the Catharist contempt for the Crucifixion, which is one reason why many think the Cathars and the Templars were closely linked. This idea seems to be confirmed by the fact that the names of several Cathar nobles were found on the Templars' roll of members. Added to this the text of the *Perlesvaus* is mystical and in places appears to support Gnostic ideas. One example is when Arthur witnesses the Mass of the Virgin, and also five 'changes of the Grail'. There is also a battle between the Fisher King and his brother, the King of Castle Mortal, symbolic of the battle between the flesh and the spirit.

# The Templars in Parzival

Although the connection between the Templars and the Grail is only speculative in the *Perlesvaus*, the text that unquestionably links the two is *Parzival*, a bold and exuberant version of the Grail story written by the German author Wolfram von Eschenbach around 1200 CE. The nature of the Grail was in debate even at that time, and Wolfram depicts it as a sacred stone. He also claimed that Chrétien de Troyes was ignorant of the real meaning of the 'Gral', but that he himself had received the true story from 'Kyot the Provencale'. Some scholars believe Kyot is a fictional character, but

others have identified him as Guiot of Provence, a troubadour and possibly a Templar initiate.

In Wolfram's text the Templars are specifically named as guardians of the Grail. They are the chosen ones who are nourished by it and who guard it on Munsalvaesche, the Mount of Salvation. He says:

> ...many formidable fighting-men dwell at Munsalvaesche with the Gral. They are continually riding out on sorties in quest of adventure. Whether these same Templars reap trouble or renown, they bear it for their sins. A warlike company lives there. I will tell you how they are nourished. They live from a Stone whose essence is most pure. If you have never heard of it I shall name it for you here. It is called 'Lapsit exillis'. By virtue of this Stone the Phoenix is burned to ashes, in which he is reborn. Thus does the Phoenix moult its feathers! Which done, it shines dazzling bright and lovely as before!...This Stone is also called 'The Gral'.[14]

The term *lapsit exillis* has puzzled many scholars. Some read it as *lapsit ex caelis*, a stone falling from the heavens, others identify it as *lapis elixir*, the alchemical Philosopher's Stone which 'turned all to gold'. Alchemists believed that this stone had healing properties and could also bestow eternal life and youth on the possessor. Certainly the image of the phoenix rising from its ashes is a familiar one in alchemy. In his actual description of the Grail procession, however, Wolfram is more allusive. He speaks of a large translucent stone which is carried in front of the Grail. The Grail itself he does not describe, except to say that it is 'the consummation of heart's desire, its root and blossoming...paradisal, transcending all earthly perfection'.[15] It is carried by the Princess of the Grail family, who wears a dress of Arabian silk. Her name is given as Repanse de Schoye (Chosen Response).

# Eastern origins

The alchemical associations hinted at in this passage and elsewhere have given rise to the idea that the Grail represents the Hermetic Vessel used in alchemy. But besides alchemy, Wolfram's *Parzival*

also contains allusions to other Eastern spiritual sciences such as astrology, astronomy, and the Kabbala. Added to this, half-way through the text he breaks off to announce that Kyot, the man who told him the tale, found it in Toledo in an Arabic script.

This script had originally been written long before the birth of Christ by a Jew named Flegetanis who was descended from Solomon. Flegetanis was an astronomer who discovered the Grail in the secrets of the stars. He declared that spiritual beings brought it to earth and withdrew again. Afterwards it came into the care of a body of worthy Christians 'bred to a pure life'. On hearing this story Kyot went looking for the men who were custodians of the Grail and found them in France.

This further reference to the Templars is followed by a reminder that in this Grail account Parzival's mother is a dark-skinned Eastern queen. Parzival also has a piebald younger half-brother named Feirefiz whom he has never met. At the end of the story they fight each other without realizing they are related. Fortunately they discover each other's identity before either is killed. After this, Cundrie the sorceress reappears and addresses Feirefiz in Christian terms and Parzival in astronomical ones. She asks their forgiveness and offers to make amends for her former anger. Then the two brothers set out to achieve the Grail together. Parzival asks the question and becomes the next Grail King with Condwiramors (Blancheflor in Chrétien's story) as his queen. Although Feirefiz is at first unable to see the Grail because he has not been baptized, this is put right and he ends up actually marrying the Grail Maiden, Repanse de Schoye. (From this unexpected liaison the enigmatic Prester John is born; see Chapter 7.)

The fact that Wolfram gives the name Chosen Response to the Grail Maiden suggests that he is concerned to unite heathen and Christian through their response to the Grail. In this he may be reflecting the attitude of the Templars themselves. Although they were fierce and faithful fighters, they began to respect and adopt Eastern wisdom and learning. It is even possible that the germ of the Grail story came from the East and was brought to Europe by the Templars, as well as the Grail itself.

# application

## The wisdom of alchemy

Jung considered that alchemy formed a link between the Gnostics and twentieth-century depth psychology. Although alchemy has been discredited by charlatan practitioners who tried to use it as a means of making gold, the true alchemist considered his work to be a bridge between the earthly and spiritual planes. The questor might find that an appreciation of the fundamental philosophy of alchemy leads to a deeper understanding of the Grail mysteries.

Wolfram von Eschenbach describes the Grail as a stone with magical properties. This has been thought to refer to the Philosophers' Stone which was said to turn base matter into gold. This is allegorical as much as chemical, the gold symbolizing the final transformation of matter into spirit.

The process by which this was thought to be attained is an extremely skilled and complex one. First the *materia prima*, or base material, has to be mixed with the First Agent, or secret fire. Both have to be prepared and purified before they can be mixed together. One represents the feminine principle of mercury, the other the masculine sulphuric principle. The two materials are then enclosed in the Philosophic Egg, a hermetically sealed vessel which is activated by a constant external heat. The materials interact, at first corrupting each other, which is described as a death. This is followed by a process of decay and corruption and issues in the black liquid *nigredo*. This phase eventually ends when a starry aspect appears, caused by the properties of mercury reasserting themselves. An intensification of heat applied at this time gives rise to a beautiful array of colours called the Peacock's Tail, which symbolizes resurrection. The colours eventually blend into a whiteness called *albedo*. But this is not the end. The *albedo* undergoes a strengthening process and turns red. This stage is known as the Red King or the Red

Rose. Eventually the whole 'work' produces the Philosophers' Stone.

From this brief account it can be seen that the Holy Grail, although depicted as a stone in *Parzival* and in this way made symbolic of the alchemical process, can also in its more usual chalice shape represent the Hermetic Vessel which contained the Materia Prima. The spear would then represent the masculine principle of the secret fire. The two interacting together chemically undergo a symbolic death and resurrection, emerging in a transcendent form.

The deep truths that alchemy seeks to represent cannot be found in linear or logical thinking. Like the Grail itself, its language is

symbolic. An insight into the secret knowledge of alchemy can be gained by a contemplation of some of its many detailed pictures or engravings. Often these depict the different stages of the 'work'.

Relax and clear your mind of all logical or intellectual thinking. Contemplate the picture below and let the symbols speak to your unconscious self.

*The Mercury of the Philosophers*

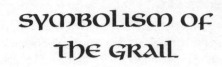

# SYMBOLISM OF THE GRAIL

All questors are aware of the significance of the symbolism surrounding the Grail. This extends to the objects, colours, landscape and people connected with it. This chapter offers some clues to a greater understanding of that symbolism. It can also be regarded as a useful consolidation of information from previous chapters.

## The Four Elements

The importance of these has been examined in Chapter 2 in relation to the four great treasures of the Celts. The theory of the Four Elements underlies all later philosophical, alchemical, scientific and mystical thinking. It was accepted by the three great religions – Christianity, Islam and Judaism – and an attempt was made to unite them on this basis.

# The Spear

The spear was originally the Spear of Lightning and one of the four Celtic Hallows. It later became identified with the lance with which the centurion Longinus pierced Christ's side while on the Cross, releasing blood and water which were caught in the Grail Chalice by Joseph of Arimathea. It was also the lance which Balin used to deal the Dolorous Stroke and maim King Pelles. During the First Crusade it was supposedly discovered at Antioch after a monk was told of its whereabouts in a dream. Its discovery heartened the Christians and helped them achieve victory in this Crusade. After this it became a sacred relic. Hitler later became obsessed with this relic, believing it bestowed invincibility on its owner.

Symbolically the spear denotes masculinity. In connection with the Grail it is seen as a symbol of male fertility. It is related to the rays of the sun and therefore of fire, and symbolizes the action of Being on Matter. The drops of blood dripping from the spear, if introduced into the Grail, regenerate the Matter within it. In the Grail legend the spear is the instrument both of affliction and of healing.

# The Round Table

The Round Table was Guinevere's marriage gift to Arthur, and previously belonged to her father. Originally, however, it was made by Merlin for Arthur's father, King Uther. It arrived with a hundred knights. Arthur was delighted and appointed Merlin to choose a further fifty knights for it. The names of the chosen knights appeared in gold letters over the seats, but at that time two were left empty. The Round Table symbolized the round world and cosmic order. The breaking up of it, which Arthur foresaw at the outset of the Grail quest, brought disharmony and disorder to the kingdom.

The Round Table is inextricably connected with the Grail legends, not least because the Holy Grail first appears in the middle of it in order to provoke the Quest for its mysteries. But there is an account

which connects the Round Table even more directly to the Grail. Robert de Boron says that Joseph of Arimathea was inspired by the Holy Spirit to set up a Table of the Grail modelled on the Table of the Last Supper. Because Judas left early to betray Jesus, a place was always left empty at the Grail Table. This table was in turn the model for the Round Table, and Judas's seat became the *Siege Perilous*, or Dangerous Seat, that could only be occupied by the perfect hero. According to Malory, the Round table held 150 knights, the same number as went on the Grail quest.

# Gwenddolau's chessboard

This is a magic chessboard, one of the Thirteen Treasures of Britain, guarded by Merlin. It belonged to the pagan King Gwenddolau, who was killed in a great battle with a Christian King. His board was said to be extremely beautiful, made of gold and silver. It was mystical in that the pieces could play by themselves. Perceval plays against them in *Peredur*. He loses and throws the board into a lake in anger. He later has to recover it under the direction of the Black Woman. Gawain also encounters this chessboard, on one occasion using it as a shield. In Celtic myth this boardgame was called *gwyddbwyll*, or *fidchell* in Ireland.

Chess also has oriental origins. It came to Spain and France via the Arabs, who respected it on two levels. It offered valuable training in terms of military strategy, and possessed mystical and symbolic properties. For example, the Queen is the most powerful piece. She can move in any direction and can overcome any opponent. She is nothing less than the Empress of the Board, having the same powers as all the other pieces except the knights. The board itself is thought to symbolize the land. In *Peredur* the chessboard is under the protection of the Black Lady but belongs to the Empress. This magical board is a persistent motif in both the Arthurian and the Grail legends.

# The Fisher King

The Fisher King was the guardian of the Grail. The fish was an ancient symbol of spirituality. The Celts believed that the oldest and wisest creature was the Salmon of Knowledge that lived at the bottom of the Well of Wisdom. Anyone lucky enough to catch and eat it would be imbued with wisdom and prophetic powers. The fish also symbolized life and fertility. It became the symbol for Christ, the Greek letters in *Ichthus* (Fish) being also the chief Greek letters for *Jesus Christ God's Son Saviour*. The symbol of the fish was therefore widely used by the early Christians. Christ was also known as the Fisher of Men. The Fisher King could therefore be seen as an ancient King of wisdom and fertility and also as Christ.

In one of the Grail stories an attempt is made to explain the Fisher King. He is said to be Brons, brother-in-law to Joseph of Arimathea, and to have caught a single fish which fed all the Grail company. The name Brons also suggests a link to the Celtic god Bran (see Chapter 2). In yet another account the Fisher King is Joseph of Arimathea himself. Elsewhere he is known as King Pelles, or Pellam. He is sometimes identified with the Maimed King who languishes from a wound in the thighs, or genitals, which also causes barrenness in the land.

# Pelles or Pellam (see also the Fisher King, above)

Pelles is King of Corbenic, the Grail Castle. He is father of Elaine, the Grail bearer, and connives in her plot to seduce Lancelot. He is also the one to receive the Dolorous Stroke from Balin. In some accounts Pelles is the son of Pellam. In others, the two are confused.

# Garlon

Garlon is the brother of King Pelles. He is the invisible knight, also called black-faced. Symbolically he is the unconscious shadow-side of the King. The black magician, Clinschor (or Klingsor) in *Parzival*, is also thought to be linked to him, as is the King of Castle Mortal who is brother to the Fisher King in the *Perlesvaus*.

# The Waste Land

This was the land ruled over by the Fisher King, also sometimes called the Maimed King. The land was laid waste by the Dolorous Stroke which rendered the King infertile. Both would be healed when the Grail hero appeared and asked the correct question. The implication is that the land was once paradisal and now needs a hero to restore it. The Land is linked to the Sovereign in Celtic myth. The Sovereign needs a healthy King or consort in order to regenerate the land. In the Grail legends the Waste Land suffers from sterility on both a physical and spiritual level. Spiritual sterility occurs when religion becomes devoid of feeling or direct experience. This parched land awaits the hero who will 'free the waters', and release the feminine powers of regeneration.

# The Castle of Corbenic

This is the Grail Castle. Corben means crow, so the castle has been identified with Dinas Bran, also known as Crow Castle, near Llangollen in Wales. Both the location and the link with the god Bran are suggestive in this respect. In the legends the Grail Castle mysteriously appears and disappears but before the rape of the Damsels of the Wells it was always visible. Symbolically, therefore, it is related to the powers of the feminine and to the land.

# The Grail Maiden

Elaine, the daughter of King Pelles, is the usual bearer of the Grail. Together with the powerful sorceress Dame Brisen, and with the connivance of her father, she tricks Lancelot into fathering Galahad by her. Instead of being angry, Lancelot recognizes that she is possessed of unusual wisdom. She is, therefore, the wise mother of the Grail hero.

In almost all accounts the Grail bearer is female. She is linked to the Damsels of the Wells who once offered drinks in golden cups to travelling knights. She is guardian of the Water of Life. In Wolfram's *Parzival* the Grail bearer is an Eastern Princess named Repanse de Schoye, or Chosen Response. This brings her to a point of identification with the Grail itself.

# Feirefiz

In Wolfram's *Parzival* Feirefiz is Parzival's half-brother. He is 'dazzlingly elegant' but also piebald, being the offspring of a black Eastern Queen and a white father. He is a noble hero because of his service of Love. He is the heathen brother to the Christian hero. He makes the correct response to the Grail Maiden and marries her. His mottled skin may symbolize the dualism inherent in the Catharist faith, as well as the mingling of East and West.

# Prester John

Wolfram says Prester John was the offspring of Feirefiz and Repanse de Schoye, and thus cousin to Arthur. This was a bold stroke to explain a strange character.

In 1145 rumours began circulating of a rich and powerful Christian King who ruled a country somewhere near India. In 1165 letters

were received by top potentates in the West from this same King, calling himself 'John, priest by the Almighty power of God' and assuring them of his extensive lands and wealth and of the Christianity of his kingdom. The Crusaders were heartened by news of such a monarch who would be a powerful ally in their cause. However, his identity was never ascertained. Marco Polo claimed to have met a monarch bearing the same title. Others say he was Genghis Khan. He is also said to be linked with the Nestorian Church. Another theory is that he was descended from the Magi. He remains a mysterious figure and some Grail seekers have claimed him on an inner level as a Grail keeper for today.

# The Ship of Solomon

*And had he set the sail, or had the boat*
*Become a living creature clad with wings?*[16]

This is the ship on which the three Grail heroes sail, guided by Dindrane, Perceval's sister. They find an extraordinary bed on it which is made from the Tree of Life and which once belonged to King Solomon. On the bed is the half-drawn sword of David. Dindrane makes new girdles for the sword (see Chapter 4).

Several ships feature in the final stages of the Grail quest. Lancelot and Galahad spend six months on one, and Dindrane is found lying dead in another. They symbolize the means of transportation from this world to that of the spirit. Perceval is taken to several islands which are reminiscent of the Celtic Otherworld.

# Sarras

This is the 'holy' city where the three main Grail heroes finally arrive, directed there by Christ in order to receive a fuller experience of the powers of the Grail. It is the place where Galahad is made King and rules for a year. Both Galahad and Dindrane are buried there and, in one account, Perceval is too. It is thought to be located somewhere on the borders of Egypt. Even though it is a pagan city, it is called holy in the texts. The fact that the Grail has to go to the East to be fully experienced suggests an acknowledgement of the importance of Eastern religious thinking.

# The Grail chapel

This is another place where the Grail can be witnessed. But in this setting it is stripped of some of its Celtic accoutrements, such as the procession, the feast and the company. The Grail chapel offers a pared-down, more obviously Christian experience. It is presided over by a hermit rather than a king. However, it is often used to give a foretaste of the final Grail experience; for example, when Lancelot sees a wounded knight being healed, presumably in token of the Maimed King's experience (See Chapter 4).

In general, the Grail chapel offers a welcome oasis of light in the middle of a dark place. It is located either in a deep forest or, in the case of the Perilous Chapel, in a dark and fearful cemetery haunted by ghostly black knights. There is another chapel of this kind in *Perlesvaus* in which Arthur and his knights have to fight off black

knights who turn into demons until the chapel can be exorcized and sanctified again.

# Dermits

The hermits maintain the holiness and sanctuary of the chapels. They provide places of healing for wounded knights and also act as spiritual advisers to questing knights. They can also be seen as the last guardians of Celtic Christian belief. In *Parzival* the hermit Trevrizant is brother to the Fisher King and therefore related to Joseph of Arimathea. The most prominent Grail hermit, Nacien, presumed to look too closely into the Grail and was blinded. His sight was restored by three drops of blood from the lance. This shows that the hermit, although a wise guide, is not the Grail hero and therefore does not have the right to experience the Grail fully.

# Saint Bernard of Clairvaux

Founder of the Order of Cistercian monks. He also wrote the Rule for the Order of Knights Templars. A very charismatic man, he inspired the second crusade with his preaching. As a child he had been taken to see the Black Virgin of Chatillon and received the miraculous grace – three drops of milk issuing from her breast. He was profoundly affected by this. As a consequence, the huge numbers of abbeys built by his Order were all dedicated to the Virgin Mary. He wrote 300 sermons on the Song of Songs and generally promoted veneration of the female through his adoration of the Virgin Mary. The Cistercian Order was instrumental in promoting the Arthurian legends, especially that of the Grail, in the *Vulgate Cycle*, their vast compilation of Arthurian literature.

# The Cailleach

Originally an ancient Celtic goddess and Earth Mother. She is the Hag of Winter and often has a blue face. As the seasons change she becomes younger and more beautiful. She is also the Hag of Beare or the Dark Lady, being the dark face of Sovereignty, the Queen of the land. She often appears in her hag-like guise and tests the hero, usually demanding a kiss or a more binding demonstration of love before revealing her true beauty. The Loathly Lady whom Gawain was obliged to marry was a type of Cailleach. She turned into a beautiful woman when he had pledged himself to her and acknowledged her sovereignty. The Cailleach challenges all who enter the Grail quest. The gift of discernment is important in dealing with her. Apparent beauty or ugliness can be deceptive. She is the bestower of wisdom and the gift of kingship.

# The Castle of Maidens

In Welsh tradition the Castle of Maidens was located at Gloucester, and in Scottish tradition, at Edinburgh. In the *Vulgate Cycle* Galahad comes upon it by the River Severn. He rescues the maidens inside by killing the seven knights who hold them prisoner. Allegorically they have been considered to be the Seven Deadly Sins and the castle to be Hell. Galahad's mission is a re-enactment of the descent of Christ into Hell to release the souls of the righteous, which here are represented by the Maidens.

Another version of the Castle of Maidens is found underwater. An example is the underwater palace where Lancelot is brought up by the Lady of the Lake. This is also a type of Otherworldly island. In Celtic myth a hero could be lured away to such a place by a beautiful maiden. Castles, walled towns, enclosed gardens and underwater islands are all aspects of the Otherworld, which can be seen as a realm where great treasures are located. It is also a place of enchantment from which it is almost impossible to escape. Heroes who enter are tempted to stay and risk losing their fighting prowess.

In Arthurian legend there are many other Castles containing Maidens that appear to be in genuine distress. These are all versions of the Castle of the Maidens found by Galahad. But in these other castles the hero is lured inside and imprisoned by the maidens. This happens with Lancelot and Morgan le Fey, and to Bors, who is entertained in a castle and tempted sexually by its Lady.

The Maidens of the castle are often faery beings, enchantresses or sorcerers as well as hapless women in need of rescuing. Psychologically they are symbols of the *anima*, the feminine aspect or soul of a man. The anima has both positive and negative aspects and it is the hero's task to rescue and transform his own 'inner feminine'.

# The number nine

Nine is the mystical number associated with women in the Grail legends. The Celts had a high regard for the number as their goddesses were often depicted in threes, symbolizing the mother, maiden and crone motif. Three times three being nine, this number was especially powerful. In Celtic legend to go beyond the ninth wave was to go beyond the known land, perhaps to where the Otherworld began.

Nine was especially associated with companies of mysterious women. The Cauldron which was kept in the Otherworldly realm of Annwn was warmed by the breath of nine priestesses. There are correspondingly nine witches whom Arthur and his men kill at the end of *Peredur*. (They are numbered in the story). There were nine druidesses on the Isle de Sein who tended the souls of the dead. There were also nine orders of angels according to esoteric Christianity and, in Greek mythology, nine muses.

# APPLICATION

## USING THE TAROT

Some truths are too deep to be expressed in words. They can be understood better in the form of symbols. The Cathars knew this and it is thought by some that they created the Tarot as a symbolic form of their beliefs. (The *Marseilles* deck is considered one of the oldest.) Certainly the figures of the Hermit, the Magician and the Pope suggest this.

Some of the older decks have been reproduced and their symbolism is obviously closer to the original meanings. At the same time, their imagery is often very detailed and will repay study. There are also many modern and imaginative decks which honour the ancient wisdom of the cards.

The Tarot should never be used as a cheap fortune-telling game; it is intended as a gateway to a deeper understanding of spiritual truths. Listed below are some of the images in the Major Arcana, with suggestions as to their Catharist meanings. A reappraisal of the Tarot in this light will make using it a richer experience and will link it to the symbolic language of the Grail. Instead of a spread, try using a single-card reading. This will help you focus more fully on some of the deeper meanings involved.

**The Fool** represents the seeker after inner knowledge.

**The Magician**, like the Alchemist, represents the inner process of transformation.

**The High Priestess** is the mystical feminine principle of wisdom and insight.

**The Empress** represents female sovereignty and motherhood.

**The Hierophant** is Pope or Initiator. Represents religious doctrine.

**The Lovers** are the highest union of male and female, leading to transformation.

**The Hermit** is a wise guide and understands the loneliness of the spiritual quest.

**The Hanged Man** offers a different perspective, a more intuitive spirituality.

**Death** denotes great change, preparation for a new emotional or spiritual beginning.

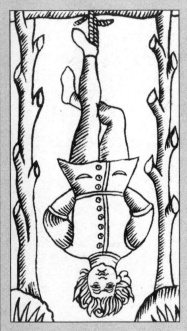

*The Hanged Man*

**Temperance** is the Grail Maiden pouring out the Water of Life, creating balance.

**The Devil** is the Magician in reverse, misusing power egotistically.

**The Tower** denotes a breaking free from old constraints of habits or beliefs.

**The Moon** is the unconscious, the female energies of the earth, the dark mother.

**The Sun** is conscious masculine energy, achievement and satisfaction.

**The World** is wholeness, synthesis, transcendence and completion.

# ΤΗΕ QUEST
# CONTINUES

*For all my blood danced in me, and I knew*
*That I should light upon the Holy Grail.*[17]

Down the centuries there has been continual speculation
concerning the Grail. Interest in it became particularly strong in
the nineteenth century when writers and artists, most notably
Tennyson and the Pre-Raphaelites, returned to the Arthurian legends
for inspiration. In the main they based their work on Malory's *Morte
d'Arthur*, which had long been considered the classic text.
Nevertheless, Tennyson in his great work *Idylls of the King* moved
away from Malory when he came to write the section on the Holy
Grail. Here he chose to follow the 'real man' *Percivale*, rather than
the idealized Galahad of Malory's story.

Tennyson's poem cuts deep because he seems to be undecided as to
whether the quest of the Grail is a glorious or an illusory one. In it
Arthur warns his knights that they may be following 'wandering
fires' rather than achieving helpful deeds of chivalry. His kingdom

suffers from the effects of so many knights leaving to go on the quest and the poem ends with Arthur questioning the nature of spiritual vision.

While Tennyson was writing his *Idylls*, Wagner was composing his opera *Parsifal*. Not surprisingly, this was inspired by Wolfram von Eschenbach's German text, *Parzival*. Since then artists and Grail-seekers have increasingly moved towards this more mystical and esoteric text. This is because it is informative on a physical as well as a spiritual level. By associating it firmly with the Templars, Wolfram provided a strong historical starting-point for seekers of the Grail as a physical artefact. Not all seekers, however, were inspired by the highest motives.

# Ḣitler's abortive quest

Directly inspired by Wagner's opera, Adolph Hitler was one of the first to attempt to find the physical Grail. He had already acquired a relic thought to be the Lance of Longinus which was found at Antioch in the First Crusade, and which he believed gave him unearthly power. Now he wanted the Grail itself. He sent Otto Rahn to the Cathar stronghold of Montségur to search the numerous caves below the mountain for the Grail, which Rahn believed was the emerald stone that had fallen to earth from Lucifer's crown, as suggested in *Parzival*. Rahn became obsessed, using geomancy and hermetic theories in his search but he was ultimately unsuccessful.

Rudolf Hess, the deputy Nazi leader, is also thought to have been sent after the Grail by Hitler, this time to Rosslyn Chapel near Edinburgh. Hess defected while on his quest and Hitler retaliated by sending many Freemasons and astrologers to concentration camps. Later he sent a further team to Montségur in a last desperate attempt to find the Grail, believing its powers would prevent the reconquest of France by the Allies. But this quest for the Grail as a source of unholy power failed.

# The Grail as Bloodline

The German mystic and founder of Anthroposophy, Rudolph Steiner, was also drawn to the Grail legends. He distinguished between *exoteric* or outward Christianity (that of the Church) and *esoteric* Christianity, an inner wisdom which ran back through mystical societies like the Theosophists, the Rosicrucians and the Freemasons to the Templars and the Cathars. He was drawn to the European and Nordic mysteries rather than to those of the East. His pupil Walter Stein wrote a book *World History in the Light of the Grail* in 1928 in which he came up with a curious but compelling new theory concerning the Grail. It is thought that ideas from this book may have been the inspiration behind the studies of Michael Baigent, Richard Leigh and Henry Lincoln, whose controversial book *The Holy Blood and the Holy Grail* exploded onto the world in 1982, provoking a new and passionate interest in the Grail.

In their book, the three authors put forward the theory that the *Sangrail* or *Sangreal* (an alternative term for the Grail) represented a royal bloodline and should be read as *Sang Real*, Royal Blood. They claim that Jesus was a Nazarite (a member of an esoteric religious sect), that he married Mary Magdalene, and that the Holy Grail that she brought to France was in fact their child carried in her womb.

They further suggest that this bloodline became allied with the royal line of the Franks, giving rise to the extraordinary Merovingian dynasty of priest-kings which ruled France in the fifth and sixth centuries. So sacred and magical was this line that the Pope made a pact with them which was later broken with the assassination of Dagobert II in 679. Dagobert's son escaped to Languedoc and the authors suggest that his line continued there and ended in Godfroi de Bouillon, founder of the mysterious order, the Priory of Sion, which was closely connected to the Templars.

# Beneath the Temple of Solomon

In fact the Templars seem to hold the key to all the recent speculations concerning the true nature of the Grail. The mysteries surrounding their secret rites and their guardianship of a sacred object are at the heart of it. We have already seen how they might have received the Holy Grail from the Cathars just before the fall of Montségur (see Chapter 5), but there is another route by which they might have come to possess a sacred object.

As noted in Chapter 6, when the Templar Order was first formed, its nine members spent nine years on the site of the ancient Temple of Solomon, without increasing their numbers. If they were supposed to be guarding travelling pilgrims then they were hardly in a position to do so effectively. So what were they doing for those nine years? Some have suggested that they were searching the Temple Stables, a vast system of man-made vaults and corridors beneath the Temple, for a well-hidden treasure left there after the siege of Jerusalem in 70 CE. If they did find an important treasure, this could explain their sudden rise in wealth and status as well as the mystery that continued to surround them.

Whether they discovered something of great value in this way, or whether they were entrusted with a sacred treasure by the Cathars is still not known. Nevertheless many researchers now believe such a treasure exists and have begun speculating on its nature. Taking their clue from the Templars' strange rituals, they even believe they may finally be on its track.

# The Templars Mysteries

Two of the most offensive confessions made by the Templars, albeit under torture, were that they worshipped an idol called Baphomet and that they required initiates to revile and spit on the Cross.

Baphomet has been described as a jewelled skull or a bearded human head. This description is based on the following entry in the list of charges made against them in 1308:

> *Being that in each province they had idols, namely heads. That they adored these idols, that they said the head could save them. That it could make riches, make the trees flower, and make the land germinate.*

The idea of a head having the mystical property to cause the land to germinate harks back to the oldest account of the Grail story, *Peredur*, in which the revered object is a severed head on a dish. It also relates to the power of the Grail being able to restore health to the land. The motif of the severed head is a strong one in Arthurian legend. It begins with such famous beheadings as that in *Gawain and the Green Knight* and extends through Chrétien to the 150 sealed heads in *Perlesvaus*.

In much of the recent speculation concerning the Grail, the idea of its being a head, or an image of a head, has been prominent. First the idea of its being the Head of Christ on the Turin Shroud was put forward, then the severed head of John the Baptist was suggested and, most recently, and most shockingly, Keith Laidler has made a leap from these suggestions to the idea that the Holy Grail is the actual mummified head of Christ, kept hidden down the centuries, but guarded and worshipped by a succession of secret sects, including the Templars.

He bases this astonishing claim not only on the confessions of the Templars but also on a Grail account which says that Nicodemus carved a likeness of Jesus's head that was so real it was 'as if God himself made it'. He puts this together with the fact that Nicodemus accompanied Joseph of Arimathea to Jesus's tomb and took with him a hundred pounds of spices, which must have been for embalming. Also, according to legend, Nicodemus was one of the company who sailed to France with Joseph of Arimathea and Mary Magdalene, who are said to have brought the Grail with them.

If either or both theories concerning Jesus's bloodline or his head were found to be true, the implications would be staggering. The authors of these speculative books are very much aware of the

shocking nature of their findings, and that proof is needed to support their theories. They realize this means finding the Grail itself, be it an actual artefact or a scroll containing documentary evidence. Many of them, however, believe they are hot on the trail and that this discovery could be within reach.

Although the theories diverge, it is remarkable how many of them locate the Grail in the same place, namely Rosslyn Chapel, near Edinburgh. But to find out why this may be the final hiding-place of the Grail we must go back in time to when the Templars hurriedly escaped with their treasure, setting sail from La Rochelle on the west coast of France.

# The hidden Grail

In 1307, twenty-four knights hurriedly set out in eighteen ships loaded with Templar treasures. Officially they disappeared, but it is known that at least one contingent arrived on the west coast of Scotland. There the Templars met up with their allies, the powerful St Clairs, whose family seat was at Roslin, near Edinburgh. At that time Scotland was independent of the Pope's jurisdiction due to the excommunication of Robert the Bruce, so it offered a safe home for the knights and their treasure. In this way, it is believed, the Grail passed into the keeping of the St Clair family. This idea seems to be confirmed by the fact that in 1446 William St Clair decided to build the curious and remarkable Rosslyn Chapel, known as the Chapel of the Grail.

## application

### The secret message of Rosslyn Chapel

Rosslyn is a place of secrets. It puzzles and intrigues the Grail-seeker with its arcane symbolism and mystical atmosphere.

Nothing can replace the physical experience of being inside this astonishing building, but a visualization is offered for those who cannot make the journey.

## Visualization

As you approach this small chapel you notice how eccentric and heavy its architecture is. Coming closer you see it is flanked with an array of massive buttresses which end at the facsimile of a ruined wall. The wall was copied from Solomon's Temple.

Entering the chapel you see at once that the stonework is covered with carvings. At first glance they appear to be Christian, but then you notice the face of a Green Man looking down from an archway, a horned devil peering from a pillar, a strange winged creature hanging upside down and bound by ropes. Above you the roof is a mass of decorations – daisies, lilies, roses and stars banded by sculpted arches. You look up at the rose window on the west wall and see that it is filled with an engrailed (scalloped) cross. This engrailed cross, which appears elsewhere, on shields and carvings, is the cross of the St Clairs. Walking around the chapel you notice a small but distinctive Templar tomb belonging to one of the many Williams of the St Clair family.

Looking towards the altar you see it is flanked by two great pillars. These represent the two great pillars of the Temple of Solomon, the priestly *Jachin* and the kingly *Boaz*. Jachin is formed of delicate columns interspersed with vertical bands of ornate patterned carving. Boaz, by contrast has a large fluted central column spiralled round with bands of winding foliage.

According to a story connected with these two columns, after carving Jachin, the master mason went on holiday. While he was away his apprentice was inspired to carve the spiralling pillar, Boaz. However, when the master mason returned he was jealous of his apprentice's accomplishment and struck him such a blow that he killed him. Thereafter Boaz has always been referred to at the *Apprentice Pillar*. It is now thought that this story was

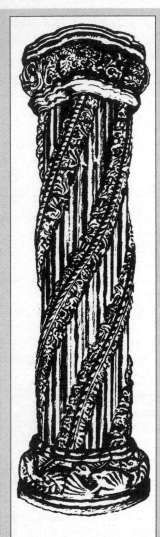

*The Apprentice Pillar at Rosslyn Chapel*

invented as a cover for an older story which is found in Freemasonry. It tells how Hiram Abif, a stonemason who worked on Solomon's Temple, was killed by a blow to the head because he would not divulge his secret knowledge to his apprentices.

Whether these stories are true or not, what is certain is that they demonstrate a link between the Holy Land, the Knights Templars and the Freemasons. In fact a close study of the stone carvings shows that pagan, Celtic and Masonic symbolism are all represented here. What the story also does is draw attention to the two pillars. However, the Mason's Pillar was plastered over for years to obscure the connection with Solomon's Temple, while the Apprentice Pillar has always been the focus of the chapel.

To the right of the Apprentice Pillar are steps going down to the crypt. It is dark and cold here with some strange drawings on the walls. It is said that at one time a figure of the Black Madonna was enshrined here. After a while you return to the chapel above. Looking around again you notice on the high altar a wooden cross with the head of Christ in the middle of it. There is so much to see and decipher, so many symbols and clues, that you almost feel overwhelmed. You realize you could spend hours here and still have new carvings to examine.

Returning finally to the Apprentice Pillar you notice a band of strange Nordic serpents coiled around its base. Could this pillar be symbolic of the *Yggdrasil*, the World Tree of Norse mythology? You stand before it, seeking to penetrate its mysteries. Is the Holy Grail hidden within this pillar, as some believe, or does it lie beneath it? You know there are sealed vaults beneath the chapel that have never been excavated. Picture in your mind what you think they might reveal.

# 9 THE GRAIL TODAY

*How blessed is Kabir, that amidst this great joy*
*he sings within his own vessel.*
*It is the music of the meeting of soul with soul.*[18]

The nature of the Grail is to challenge settled views and present new ways of thinking. Down the centuries, as we have seen, it has always run counter to dogmatic belief. At the same time it seems to have had something of a love-affair with established religion. It unsettles it, but is never far from it. A strongly feminine symbol, on both a spiritual and psychological level, the Grail has always offered an alternative spirituality with the potential to enrich more masculine forms of thinking and belief.

If we put together the Grail researchers' findings, both those on a physical and on a spiritual level, we can reach a greater appreciation of the Grail's potential. The Grail has always been strongly associated with the idea of blood, not only sacramentally,

as in the blood of Christ, but also in terms of blood relations. The figure of Joseph of Arimathea has been used to suggest an alternative family of Grail guardians who are interrelated with the knights of Arthur – in particular, Perceval, Lancelot and Galahad. On a physical level this has led researchers to exciting and shocking possibilities, namely that Christ had children by the hitherto despised Mary Magdalene, and that these children were the forebears of European kings. On a spiritual one, it has taken us via the cult of the Magdalene into Gnosticism and the Feminine Mysteries.

As regards the other powerful physical and spiritual symbol, that of the severed head, it will be helpful to return to the oldest story of the Grail in existence, namely *Peredur* in the *Mabinogion*. Unlike Chrétien's unfinished story, *Peredur* depicts the Grail as a severed head, and has an ending. This ending has often been ignored by scholars because it presents so many problems. Nevertheless, a reconsideration of it in the light of our researches, may yield some further insights.

# The ending of the Grail story

At first reading the ending of *Peredur* seems completely unsatisfactory. A yellow-haired boy kneels before Peredur and admits to having been behind most of the female figures in the story, including the Black Woman and the Grail-bearer. He then says that the severed head belonged to Peredur's first cousin who was killed by the Hags of Gloucester, who also lamed his uncle. He ends by telling Peredur of the prophecy that he, Peredur, will take revenge. After this Peredur summons Arthur and his knights, who fight the hags and kill them after first giving them a chance to stop the fighting. The Hags consider themselves to be fated and keep fighting until eventually they are all killed.

# The yellow-haired boy

The first problem for the reader is that of the yellow-haired boy claiming to be most of the women in the story. The scholar Roger Sherman Loomis has come up with a possible explanation for this. He argues that the old French word for 'high-born maiden' is *damoisele*, which differs from the word for 'high-born youth', *damoisel*, by only one letter, and could account for what seems like a confusion of masculine with feminine.[19] If this were the case, then, instead of the youth, it would be a blonde-haired maiden who confessed to being both the Black Woman and Grail-bearer. This would accord with Celtic belief in the Maiden/Crone aspects of the Goddess and make the reading more satisfactory.

But even if we accept this as a reasonable explanation, there still remains the puzzle of the severed head and the Hags of Gloucester.

# The Hags of Gloucester

All we know about the Hags of Gloucester is that there were nine of them and that they were warrior women with whom Peredur had previously trained for three weeks in the skills of horsemanship. The abilities of such women are well documented in Celtic myth. Many heroes, such as the Irish Cuchulain, were trained by women and it is not inappropriate for Peredur to have received lessons from them. On a symbolic level, however, the fact that they are described as hags suggests the figure of the Cailleach, whose warrior powers made her a type of challenger.

# Priestesses of the Otherworld

In many of the Celtic and Arthurian tales the women are shown collectively, often in groups of nine. This could simply denote

communities of women or, alternatively, it could represent the tripling of the triple-aspected goddess into a single great power. Whichever it is, the number is symbolic rather than actual and represents the feminine aspect in its fullest force.

In this respect correlations can be drawn between the various mystical groups of women in the legends. For example, the nine priestesses on the *Isle de Sein* who tend the souls of the dead must surely be linked with the nine priestesses who guard the magic cauldron of Annwn. Both groups of women are priestesses and both are linked to the Otherworld. The only difference is that one group tends the souls of the departed, while the other guards the magic cauldron. But are these different?

# The Castle of Marvels

At the end of *Peredur* the reader is directed to the Fortress of Marvels. In Chrétien's story this is also called the Castle of Marvels and is inhabited by an imprisoned community of fatherless girls, disenfranchized widows and young men waiting to be knighted. Galahad breaks the spell and frees them all, knighting the young men. Then the story breaks off.

The Castle of Marvels is related to the Castle of Maidens who are also imprisoned and who are rescued by Galahad (see Chapter 7). This has been explained as an allegory in which Galahad, as a type of Christ, descends into Hell or the Otherworld and releases the imprisoned souls.

The idea of women representing the soul accords with psychological and esoteric thinking. Added to this, the various castles in the Arthurian legends have usually been viewed as types of the Otherworld. The Maidens of the Castle, therefore, are another type of collective femininity guarding the soul.

The Castle of Maidens was located near Gloucester. The nine Hags of Gloucester are connected with the Grail in the form of a severed head and they are fought by Arthur and his retinue. Therefore it may

91

be that they are the dark counterparts of the nine priestesses who guard the Grail in Annwn, whom Arthur and his Knights also fight.

# FEMININE VENGEANCE

If, as some scholars believe, there is a vengeance theme running through the stories of the Grail, this could lie in the conflict between the opposing energies of feminine and masculine principles. Whether or not the Hags of Gloucester represent the dark side of the feminine, they certainly oppose the masculine forces represented by Arthur and his knights. But at some level they know this creates imbalance and that they, in turn, are fated to be overcome.

# The severed head

The severed head forms part of the theme of feminine vegeance. In her dark aspect the feminine has severed the head of man and guards it. The head was regarded by the Celts as the seat of the soul. The dark feminine, therefore, guards the soul of man who is forced to brave her wrath in order to recover it. At the same time she acts as his challenger, deliberately provoking him into such action, knowing that her feminine energies need to be linked to male consciousness for full realization of their powers.

# Healing the Waste Land

At present the land suffers greatly from the withdrawal of feminine understanding and nurturing. It has been raped by masculine greed and desire. The dishonoured female hides and angrily withholds her wisdom. Yet she knows at some level that this is wrong. At the end of Wolfram's *Parzival*, Cundrie the Sorceress, who is treated with

respect despite her hideousness, kneels before Perceval and asks him to pardon her. Then she assists both Perceval and his brother to achieve the Grail. After this there is great happiness and rejoicing, Perceval is reunited with his wife and Feirefiz marries the Grail maiden.

Perhaps it is no accident that Wolfram's text has recently gained such popularity. His version of the Grail story speaks, on many levels, of reconciliation. As such it is clearly relevant to us today. Any belief system which favours the masculine over the feminine, or the converse, risks continual feud, continual imbalance and sickness in the individual psyche as well as in the land. Both male and female need the 'freeing of the waters' for their survival. The earth has been dishonoured and the land laid waste for too long. A truce must be called if human life is to continue. Male and female must learn to respect and honour each other's powers; they must also seek to balance their energies for the good of the earth.

Already, today, there are signs that this is beginning to happen. Male domination is being questioned and women are winning back respect and power. There is also a new awareness of the plight of the earth. At this most crucial time, it seems there is a real opportunity for healing and reconciliation at every level. This is the insight the Grail offers us today.

But the Grail never finishes with us. Even if this truce is achieved, it will demand more. The Grail is not only a symbol of balance and healing, it goes beyond reconciliation, calling mankind to the highest challenge of which it is capable. Ultimately, as Wolfram's text suggests, it requires nothing less than the mystical combustion and blending of feminine and masculine energies in its powerful matrix. Only in this way can the transformation of humanity, both psychologically and spiritually, finally be achieved.

# application

## The mystical experience

Any approach to the Grail must be made with the realization that its powers can be overwhelming. Its mystery is primarily experienced through the senses and it may be that you need to achieve it in stages. When using this visualization go only as far as you feel is appropriate.

Find a comfortable place and let your busy thoughts drop away, your mind go quiet. Imagine you are on a narrow path in a deep forest. Ahead of you is a pinpoint of light. As you approach you see it is a sanctuary. This may be a grove, a chapel, a tower, or a castle with a special room in it. As you get nearer you see it is filled with light, spilling out towards you. At the same time you become aware that you are surrounded by music. It is an outpouring of birdsong, rich and beautiful. Stop and listen to it.

When you are ready, move on towards your sanctuary. When you reach it, enter hesitantly, aware of its holiness. Ahead of you is a table and on the table a rich cloth. On the cloth is an object which is difficult to see at first because it is sending out so much light. Is it a chalice, a book, a beautiful carved stone or a jewelled crystal? As you approach, the light increases, a great fragrance fills the air and your senses are overwhelmed. Close your eyes.

Feel the light filling your head and running down your limbs. You are being washed through with light. Old problems and difficulties, old fears and darknesses are being released as new energy pours in. Stay with this experience for as long as you can. Only if you are sure you are ready, touch or pick up the object. Be careful because its power may be too strong for you at this time. If it is a stone or jewel, feel the concentration of its energy, look into its depths. What image do they contain? If it is a book, open it and see what it says. If it is a cup or chalice lift it to your

lips. Let its healing draught flow into you, its healing powers work within you. Wait until you feel the work completed, until you are at peace.

Then slowly leave your inner sanctuary and come back into this world. Remember you can return there whenever you feel the need.

Knights praying at the Grail Chapel

# REFERENCES

For more details, see Bibliography

[1] Matthews, John, *The Grail Tradition*, p. 19 (verse 2)
[2] From *The Elucidation*, quoted in Matthews, John, *Sources of the Grail*, p. 67
[3] MacNeice, Louis, *The Dark Tower*, p. 57
[4] Tennyson, *The Holy Grail* from *Idylls of the King*
[5] Robert de Boron ll. 3332–6, quoted in Cavendish, Richard, p. 148
[6] Anon, *The Quest of the Holy Grail* (Vulgate Cycle), p. 47
[7] Lalleswari or Lal Diddi of Kashmir, quoted in *The Virago Book of Spirituality*, p. 99
[8] Pagels, Elaine, *The Gnostic Gospels*, p. 84
[9] Ibid. p. 43
[10] Ibid. p. 45
[11] Layton, Bentley, *The Gnostic Scriptures*, p. 332
[12] Ibid. pp. 80–1
[13] Poeticized version of description in *Parzival*, p. 232
[14] Wolfram von Eschenbach, *Parzival*, p. 239
[15] Ibid. p. 125
[16] Tennyson, *The Holy Grail*
[17] Ibid.
[18] Kabir, *Poem XCVIII*, quoted in *One Hundred Poems of Kabir*
[19] Loomis, R.S. *The Grail – From Celtic Myth to Christian Symbol*, p. 92

# SELECT BIBLIOGRAPHY AND DISCOGRAPHY

Baigent, Leigh and Lincoln, *The Holy Blood and the Holy Grail*, Arrow Books, 1982

Begg, Ean and Deike, *In Search of the Holy Grail and the Precious Blood*, Thorsons, 1995

Bryant, M. (trans.), *The High Book of the Grail – Perlesvaus*, Brewer, 1978

Cavendish, Richard, *King Arthur and The Grail*, Book Club Assoc.,1978

Chrétien de Troyes, *Arthurian Romances*, Everyman, 1997

Coghlan, Ronan, *The Illustrated Encyclopaedia of Arthurian Legends*, Element, 1991

Gantz, Jeffrey (trans.), *The Mabinogion*, Penguin, 1976

Geoffrey of Monmouth, *The History of the Kings of Britain*, Penguin, 1966

Godwin, Malcolm, *The Holy Grail*, Bloomsbury, 1994

Jung, Emma and von Franz, Marie-Louise, *The Grail Legend*, Sigo Press, Boston, 1986

Kabir, *One Hundred Poems*, Tagore, Rabindrath (trans.), Macmillan, 1962

Laidler, Keith, *The Head of God*, Orion, 1998

Layton, Bentley, *The Gnostic Scriptures*, SCM Press, 1987

Loomis, R. S., *The Grail From Celtic Myth to Christian Symbolism*, Columbia University Press, 1963

MacNeice, Louis, *The Dark Tower*, Faber, 1947

Malory, *Le Morte D'Arthur*, vols 1 and 2, Penguin, 1969

Matarasso, P. M. (trans.), *The Quest of the Holy Grail*, Penguin, 1969

Matthews, John, *The Grail: Quest for the eternal*, Thames & Hudson, 1981

Matthews, John, *The Grail Tradition*, Element, 1990
Matthews, John, *The Mystic Grail*, Thorsons, 1997
Matthews, John, *Sources of the Grail*, Floris Books, 1996
Matthews, John and Green, Marian, *The Grail Seekers' Companion*, Aquarian Press, 1986
Pagels, Elaine, *The Gnostic Gospels*, Penguin Books, 1979
Picknett, L, and Prince, C., *The Templar Revelation*, Corgi, 1997
Sinclair, Andrew, *The Discovery of the Grail*, Arrow Books, 1999
Wallace-Murphy, T. and Hopkins, M., *Rosslyn – Guardian of the Secrets of the Holy Grail*, Element, 1999
Virago Book of Spirituality, Virago Press, 1997
Weston, Jessie, L., *From Ritual to Romance*, Cambridge University Press, 1920

# Music

Noirin Ni Riain, *Celtic Soul*, Earth Music Productions, LMUS 0031
Loreena McKennitt, *Parallel Dreams*, Quinlan Road Ltd., Canada, QRCD 103
*Celtic Woman*, (compilation), Celtic Woman Records, CWRCD 7001
Alan Stivell, *Renaissance of the Celtic Harp*, Rounder Records, Massachusetts, CD 3067

Available from C. Hamilton, c/o the publisher, or at:
**claire@hamiltonharps.freeserve.co.uk**
Company of Strangers, *Blodeuwedd – A Wife Out of Flowers*, COS 298
The Company of Strangers, *The Love-Song of Diarmuid and Grainne*, CSSM1 (cassette)
*The Celtic Harp*, Claire Hamilton, Sound and Media SUMCD 4133
*The Celtic Harp Collection*, Claire Hamilton, e2 ETD CD/003
*Celtic Myths*, Claire Hamilton (harp and spoken word), Music Collection International ETD CD/157

# INDEX

# ARThURIAN TRADITION

## Claire Hamilton

If you've a fascination with the tales of King Arthur or Queen Guinevere you'll enjoy this momentary escape into the world of Arthurian tradition. This book demonstrates the enduring power of King Arthur as guardian of the land, Grail-seeker, and model hero of the last Millennium.

- Discover the mythical hero in historical context
- Explore the strange nature of Courtly Love
- Uncover the magical and psychological significance of Merlin and Morgan Le Fay
- Delve into the tangled nature of love triangles
- Investigate the symbolism of magical objects involved in the legends

Practical applications at the end of each chapter help to consolidate each stage of the 'quest' throughout the book.

Claire Hamilton is a writer, performer and Celtic harpist. She has explored myths in all these capacities and has an MA in *The Bardic Tradition in Ireland*.

# TIMELESS WISDOM OF THE CELTS

## Steve Eddy & Claire Hamilton

This book reveals the roots of ancient Celtic wisdom and gives practical advice on how to apply it to our everyday life: our relationships and sexuality; our family; home; work; health and spirituality.

*Timeless Wisdom of the Celts* investigates the cultural and historical context of a people who emerged around the 5th century BC. Steve Eddy and Claire Hamilton look at a wealth of examples, including

* the Celts in history
* the relationship of the Celts with nature
* the role of the hero
* the Otherworld
* gods and goddesses
* the cycles of the season
* the arts
* myths and legends

The book shows how all of these topics relate to modern life, and continue to intrigue and inspire us.